NOLS COOKERY

edited by
Sukey Richard, Donna Orr, and Claudia Lindholm

Third Edition
1991

A publication of
The National Outdoor Leadership School
and
Stackpole Books

Printed in the United States of America.

Design by Tom Wright
Cover and internal dividers by Bill Petersen
Text illustrations by Joan M. Safford

First edition: 1974
Second edition: 1988
Third edition: 1991

Library of Congress Cataloging in Publication Data

NOLS Cookery.

   Includes index
   1. Outdoor cookery   I. Richard, Sukey, 1954-
II. Orr, Donna, 1945-   III. Lindholm, Claudia, 1955-
IV. National Outdoor Leadership School (U.S.)
TX823.N65 1988   641.5'78   88-60635
ISBN 0-8117-3083-2

TABLE OF CONTENTS

FROM TABLESIDE TO TRAILSIDE

For some, cooking in the backcountry is a rewarding experience; they cannot wait to stir up a favorite coffee cake, soup, or stew. With a spice kit and a few tricks of the trail, gourmet meals can result from their labors. For others, the prospect of food selection and preparation sends shivers down the spine. "How will I survive? Will I be able to carry it all? How many calories do I need? What is a high carbohydrate food? How do I know all of this can be prepared over one small stove? Where do I find the correct foods that are light-weight, appealing and nourishing?"

Meals in the wilderness can be one of the most enjoyable and controllable aspects of your outdoor experience, provided that considerable planning occurred before you ever left the safety of your own kitchen. The *NOLS Cookery* will assist you in organizing the details by giving the framework for menu development, purchasing, and preparation. In 1974 I studied Paul Petzoldt's *Wilderness Handbook* in great detail, anxiously gleaning any remarks on menus, foodstuffs, stoves, and fuel. That was the first time I saw the acronym "NOLS." Shortly afterward, the first edition of *NOLS Cookery* addressed these essential food facts in one informative, concise, pack-size booklet. For years, I have purchased the NOLS cookbook in mass quantities, sending it with each group of climbers, mountaineers, and backpackers that I counseled.

After all, careful, creative planning results in a menu based on the reality of energy expenditure, environment, equipment, time, and fuel. Familiarization with the basic four food groups will establish a foundation for all life's menus, whether in the wilderness or at home, travelling or training.

At no time in your life will you have a better opportunity to understand energy needs and caloric balance than on an wilderness expedition. Respect for nature's gifts are part of the process. Food and fuel take on new meanings: cups of melting snow become mentally measured as cups of water; fuel is projected in terms of burning time, and pounds of food are equivalent to days on the trail. This leaves more time to truly enjoy your adventure and deal with the uncontrollable details of your trip such as weather, water sources or "disappearing" trails.

There are those who will only know fine dining in fancy restaurants. How can we adequately describe to them the pleasure of a satisfying day on the trail, enhanced even more by a nourishing, tasty meal consumed beside a running stream, as the sun sets behind the silhouetted mountains? I challenge you to follow this handbook and to become a confident wilderness cook whose efficiency generates time for watching many sunsets.

Julie Ann Lickteig, M.S., Registered Dietitian
Member of the Sports and Cardiovascular Nutritionists (SCAN)
of the American Dietetic Association

INTRODUCTION

Several years ago a NOLS Instructor out on a course was approached at camp by one of her students, who complained that the cake he was baking wouldn't rise.

Oh, said the Instructor, you probably forgot the baking soda. No, the student replied, I put it in. And one by one they went through the entire list of ingredients—flour, salt, sugar, powdered milk; the student insisted he had included them all.

Well, give it more time, suggested the Instructor. But the student returned again in half an hour saying the cake still hadn't done a thing.

Curious, the instructor went to investigate and discovered the student had neglected to add—the water.

Cooking is an essential part of any outdoor experience. Here at NOLS our goal is to issue a variety of foods while keeping expenses down and also provide students with opportunities for creativity, individual choices and learning new skills. Once students have learned to prepare meals in the outdoors, they've acquired skills that will last a lifetime.

Through the years, thousands of NOLS students have faced cooking their first meal with only the slender volume NOLS Cookery to aid them. We have revised and added to the original Cookery first published in 1974. The information has been updated to reflect current NOLS rationing procedures and more up-to-date information on nutrition and conservation practices. All the recipes were tested and many new ones added.

This cookbook was designed with backpackers in mind, but the ideas suggested here would be helpful for any outdoor pursuit where weight is a factor. The conservation practices we recommend reflect the most current research on the subject and are provided as a resource for all concerned backcountry travelers.

We dedicate this new edition to the NOLS students who discovered what great cooks they could be, the NOLS instructors who encouraged them, and the thousands of great meals prepared in spectacular surroundings from Baja to Alaska, Kenya to Argentina, and in the Wind Rivers, where NOLS and NOLS Cookery had their beginnings.

Our thanks to all those individuals who have contributed to the body of knowledge represented in this new edition of NOLS Cookery. With special thanks to the original editors, Nancy Pallister and Tina Cunningham, and to Sierra Adare, Gina Baldwin, Mike Bailey, Ian Gersten, Phil Powers, Del Smith, and Lucy Smith for their recipe ideas and to anyone else who wandered into the NOLS test kitchen and said, "Well, I do it this way..."

Claudia Lindholm
Sukey Richard
Donna Orr

PLANNING

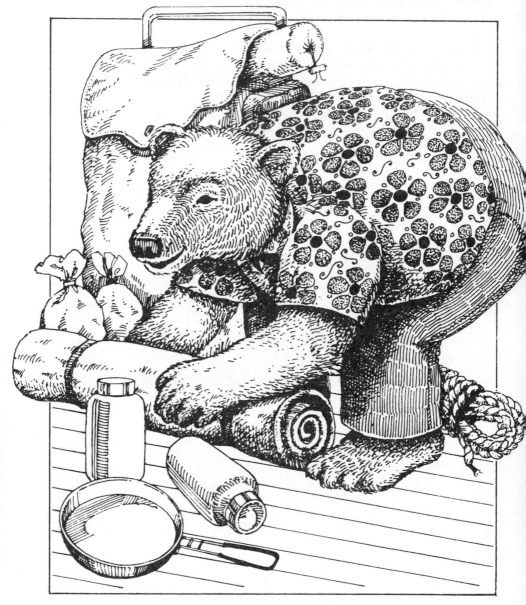

RATION PLANNING
NUTRITION AND QUANTITIES
FOOD GLOSSARY • PACKAGING
RATION RESUPPLY

RATION PLANNING

Each year approximately 2,000 students attend NOLS courses. The majority of NOLS courses last 31 days. How does the NOLS Rationing Department plan meals for so many people over so long a period? The answer is we don't. Each course is divided into cook groups of two or three individuals, each cook group being issued a wide selection of bulk foods and seasonings. It is up to the student cook groups to decide what meals they will prepare with the raw materials they are provided.

We call this method NOLS *bulk rationing* and it works very well for our extended expeditions. Smaller groups going out for shorter lengths of time might want to consider *menu planning*, where meals are planned in advance and the food bought accordingly.

Bulk rationing may be a difficult concept to grasp at first if you have always used menu planning, but the rewards can be great once you've mastered the basic concept. Planning and packing become easier. Complicated lists and menu schedules are eliminated. You'll have greater freedom in the field to prepare meals that suit your mood and the demands of the day. Cooking becomes more creative and flexible when you carry "a backcountry pantry" in your pack.

Factors you will want to consider whichever system you choose include:

- Group size
- Duration of trip
- Purpose of trip
- Exertion level
- Weather
- Altitude
- Individual appetites
- Food preferences within your group
- Nutritional balance
- Expense and availability
- Spoilage and ease of packaging
- Weight

The freeze-dried meals available at backpacking and sporting goods stores have their uses at times—when weight and time are critical factors—but they are an expensive and often tasteless luxury. If you do decide to go with freeze-dried, be forewarned that their suggested serving sizes should be doubled for most appetites. They are also extremely high in salt. Often freeze dried food used in conjunction with staples can help provide variety.

You can find many tasty, lightweight, nutritious, and inexpensive options at your local supermarket, natural foods store, or oriental market. Check to see if your grocer will special order hard to find items like tomato base and dehydrated hash browns.

Keep in mind the food preferences of your group, and beware of letting your personal likes and dislikes influence your choices too much. Remember that variety is important and will help keep morale up. Determine a budget. Balance expensive and less expensive items.

NUTRITION AND QUANTITIES

NOLS Rationing System

If you are planning a trip by the *NOLS Bulk Rationing* method, you will first need to calculate the total poundage of food you need. NOLS issues a combination of heavier "grocery store" foods and lighter dehydrated items. If you must reduce weight, diligent use of freeze-dried food can lower your overall poundage by 20-25% and produce nutritious meals.

The first step is to decide how many POUNDS of food per PERSON per DAY you need. Total poundage per day depends more on the intensity and duration of energy expenditure, age and size of participant, and less on environmental conditions such as weather or altitude.

AVERAGE WILDERNESS EXPERIENCE: IE: BACKPACKING, SKI TOURING, KAYAKING

1.5 POUNDS / 2.0 POUNDS — I PERSON — FOR 1 DAY — ROUGHLY 2500 TO 3000 CALORIES — FOR NORMAL WORKDAYS.

STRENUOUS ACTIVITIES: IE: SNOW CAMPING

2.0 POUNDS / 2.25 POUNDS — I PERSON — FOR 1 DAY — ROUGHLY 3000 TO 3700 CALORIES — FOR HEAVIER WORKDAYS

VERY STRENUOUS ACTIVITIES: IE: EXTREME MOUNTAINEERING

2.25 POUNDS / 2.5 — I PERSON — FOR 1 DAY — ROUGHLY 3700 TO 4500 CALORIES — EXTREMELY HEAVY WORKDAYS

The following sample NOLS ration illustrates how the total ration poundage can be broken down into individual food categories and quantities figured. This is intended as an example; no doubt you will want to make adjustments for your particular group's requirements. It's important to make substitutions for any items you eliminate to ensure that you include an adequate number of calories. For instance, if you eliminate flour because you don't plan to bake, be sure to substitute some prebaked goods such as crackers, bagels, or pita bread. If you don't want as much cheese, substitute canned chicken or tuna. Don't substitute coffee for cocoa since coffee has no nutritional value and cocoa is an important source of milk and calories.

SAMPLE RATION

Number of people: 2   Number of Days: 10

Pounds per person per day: 2 lbs.

Total 2 lbs. x 2 persons x 10 days = 40 lbs.

Staples:

2 lbs. margarine	1 lb. orange drink
2 lbs. powdered milk	1/2 lb. apple cider mix
1/2 lb. powdered eggs	1 lb. brown sugar
3 lbs. cocoa	3 lb. cheddar cheese
2 lbs. whole wheat flour	2 lbs. Monterey Jack cheese
1 lb. white flour	

Trail foods:

1 lb. fig bars	1/2 lb. dried apricots
1/2 lb. yogurt malt balls	1/2 lb. oat cakes
1/2 lb. trail mix	1 lb. Spanish peanuts
1/2 lb. pretzels	1/2 lb. walnuts
1 lb. raisins	1/2 lb. dates

Desserts:

1/2 lb. cheesecake	1/2 lb. brownies
1/4 lb. popcorn	

Breakfast:

1 lb. oatmeal	1 lb. Cracklin' Bran
2 lbs. dehydrated hash browns	1/2 lb. sliced potatoes
1/2 lb. instant Cream of Wheat	1 lb. granola

Dinner foods:

1 lb. macaroni	1 lb. white rice
1 lb. spinach noodles	1/2 lb. artichoke spaghetti
1/2 lb. lentils	1/2 lb. potato pearls
1/2 lb. bulgar-soy grits	1/2 lb. tortillas
1/2 lb. pinto beans	1/8 lb. beef base
1/2 lb. tomato base	1/2 lb. chicken noodle soup base
1/8 lb. vegetable cubes	1 lb. cous-cous

TOTAL   40 lbs.

Not included in weight:

Dry goods

1/3 box stick matches plus 5 books matches

20 tea bags, assorted   1 bar soap

1/2 roll toilet paper

Seasonings

1 ounce each: chili powder, curry. 2 ounces each: dehydrated onions, salt, pepper, garlic powder, Spike, vanilla, Tabasco, dried peas and carrots. 3 ounces each: dried mixed vegetables. 4 ounces each: soy sauce, oil, vinegar.

Most people do not have scales handy when re-packaging bulk foods. We have provided a list of some common backpacking foods and how many cups of dry food make up a pound.

Apples, dried, firmly packed...5 cups
Bacon bits ....6 cups
Bases ....2 1/2 cups
Baking mix, lightly packed ....3 1/2 cups
Brown sugar, firmly packed..3 1/2 cups
Cashews..3 cups
Cheese, powdered ....4 cups
Cocoa, commercial w/ non-instant milk...........................6 cups
Cocoa, home mix with instant milk ....4 1/2 - 5 cups
Coffee, freeze-dried instant ....6 cups
Cornmeal ....3 1/2 cups
Cream of Wheat..3 cups
Eggs, powdered..4 cups
Flour...3 1/2 cups
Fruit drinks, dry with sugar..3 cups
Honey..1 cup
Lentils ....3 cups
Macaroni, elbow ....4 cups
Milk, powdered instant...6 cups
Mixed vegetables, dehydrated ....6 cups
Oatmeal..5 cups
Peanuts, shelled ....3 cups
Popcorn ....2 cups
Potatoes, flake...8 cups
Pudding, dry mix ....3 cups
Raisins..4 cups
Sunflower seeds, shelled ....3 1/2 cups

It will help you in putting together your rations to have a basic understanding of nutrition. The success of your expedition and staying healthy, building up muscles, remaining warm, cheerful, and alert all depend on eating properly.

Nutritionists today recognize four basic food groups and two additional categories:

THE MILK GROUP supplies calcium, riboflavin (vitamin B2), and protein. Cheese, milk, cocoa, cheesecake, and puddings fall in this category. (2-4 servings per day)

THE MEAT GROUP supplies these key nutrients: protein, niacin, iron, and thiamin (vitamin B1) for muscle, bone and blood cells, and healthy skin and nerves. Peanut butter, eggs, beans, legumes, and nuts fall in this category. (2 servings per day)

THE FRUIT-VEGETABLE GROUP supplies these key nutrients: vitamin A and vitamin C for night vision, resistance to infections, and help in healing wounds. Potatoes, freeze-dried vegetables, tomato base, fortified fruit drinks, dried fruit, and wild edibles fall in this category. (4 servings per day)

THE GRAIN GROUP supplies carbohydrate, thiamin, iron, and niacin for energy and a healthy nervous system. Flour, pasta, rice, cereals, cous-cous, and bulgar fall in this category. (4 servings per day)

COMBINATION FOODS contain ingredients from more than one food group and supply the same nutrients as the foods they contain. Examples include: quiche, pizza, and macaroni and cheese. These count as servings (or partial servings) of the four basic food groups they contain.

OTHER FOODS complement but don't replace foods from the four basic food groups: sweets, fats and oils, coffee, tea, and condiments fall in this category. Since these foods provide additional calories beyond those contained in the basic four, amounts are determined by individual needs.

Every day you should eat a wide variety of food from the four basic food groups. By choosing different foods, you are likely to get the nutrients you need. Nutrients can be grouped into six classes:

PROTEIN is necessary to build all body cells. Since your cells are constantly being replaced, you need protein all your life. Proteins are made up of amino acids. Animal proteins (meat, cheese, milk) supply amino acids in the right proportions for your body to use. Proteins from plant foods (beans, legumes, grains) usually lack some indispensable amino acid. These foods are called *incomplete proteins*. By combining certain incomplete proteins, you can produce a complete protein for your body to use. Some successful combinations are: beans and rice, peanuts and wheat, and macaroni and cheese.

CARBOHYDRATES are the starches and sugars in foods from plants. During exercise, you burn body-stored carbohydrates. The more you exercise, the more carbohydrate-rich foods you need. A high carbohydrate diet means eating a variety of vegetables, whole grains, legumes, and fruits. These foods supply complex carbohydrates and also provide fiber. Sugar consumption is *not* necessarily synonymous with instant energy, nor is it a source of complex carbohydrates.

FATS take longer for your body to digest but will start to provide energy after the quicker burning carbohydrates have been used up.

VITAMINS have no caloric value but are essential for your body to function properly. The average person eating a balanced and varied diet does not need vitamin supplements.

MINERALS help in many physiological functions. They also come from the food you eat; some are also found in water.

WATER makes up from 1/2 to 3/4 of your body weight. Your body's need for water increases with exercise due to sweating and respiration losses. In the summer, drink a minimum of 2-3 quarts per day. In winter 3-4 quarts, and at altitude (more than 7,000 feet) 3-5 quarts. Becoming dehydrated causes headaches, muscle cramps, and nausea and can increase your susceptibility to hypothermia, frostbite, and altitude sickness.

Your energy for everything you do is obtained from the protein, carbohydrates, and fat in the food you eat. "Calories" are simply a measurement of that energy. Proteins and carbohydrates each supply roughly 112 calories per ounce. Fat is a more concentrated source of energy and supplies approximately 252 calories per ounce.

If you use more calories than you consume, you lose weight; if you consume more calories than you use, you gain.

FOOD GLOSSARY

Here we've listed some suggestions for foods that travel well and will help provide a tasty and nutritious variety on the trail.

TRAIL FOODS

Fruit

DRIED APPLES, APRICOTS, FIGS, DATES, PRUNES, MIXED FRUIT, PINEAPPLE, PEARS, PEACHES and RAISINS

Good source of bulk, fiber, carbohydrates; soaking in warm water for a short time before baking will soften and plump up fruits. These fruits last longer without refrigeration if they have been sulphured. This process helps retain color, moisture, and some minerals and vitamins. Naturally dried fruits are preferred but they darken, mold, and dry out without refrigeration. At NOLS we find sulphured fruits work best because they have to go for long periods of time under changing climatic conditions before being eaten.

Hint: Too many eaten as snacks without proper rehydration can cause stomach cramps and gas.

BANANAS and COCONUT

Great as an ingredient in trail mix, banana bread, granola, desserts, baked goods, and curry dishes; rehydrating banana chips leaches out flavor and sweetness; it's better to crush small then add to recipes.

FRUIT BARS, FRUIT POPTARTS, and GRANOLA BARS

Excellent for a change from fruits and nuts; popular and quick lunch; crumble fairly easily; can be spread with peanut butter or cream cheese; good source of carbohydrates for quick energy.

FRUIT LEATHERS

Nice tart flavor; naturally sweetened; good source of carbohydrate and vitamin C; a quick energy alternative to candy.

Crackers and Breadstuffs

FLOUR or CORN TORTILLAS

Great bread substitute for short ration periods; serve heated leftovers in lightly fried tortillas; versatile but use quickly as they can mold or go stale.

BAGELS, ENGLISH MUFFINS, PITA BREAD
A break from nuts and dried fruits; good for breakfast, lunch, or dinner with spreadables or melted cheese; quick and tasty; bulky for long rations.

MELBA TOASTS, BREADSTICKS, BAGEL CHIPS, PILOT BREAD, ZWIEBACK, OAT CAKES, ETC.
Hard, durable bread products; great with cheese.

PARTY MIX, TRAIL MIXES, SALAD GEMS, and PRETZELS
Individual items or various combinations of small crackers, nuts, dried fruits, candies, seeds, etc. specifically made for backpackers and available in grocery and natural food stores; adds welcome crunch to backpacker's diet; can go stale quickly or crumble easily.

Nuts and Seeds
ALMONDS, BRAZIL NUTS, CASHEWS, PEANUTS, MIXED NUTS, CORN NUTS, WALNUTS, PECANS, FILBERTS, SUNFLOWER SEEDS, SESAME SEEDS, PUMPKIN SEEDS
All nuts and seeds are good sources of proteins and fats; raw nuts and seeds keep indefinitely and can be pepped up by dry-roasting and seasoning right before eating; oil roasted, salted nuts and seeds start to oxidize when exposed to air and become rancid and stale; refrigeration provides the best storage for these.

Nut Butters
PEANUT, CASHEW, ALMOND, TAHINI
Popular, rich, tasty, high energy food; good on crackers and in sauces, tasty in grain or pasta dishes; very good source of fats and protein.

Candy and Sweets
CHOCOLATE PRODUCTS
M & M's, candy bars, etc.; popular as special treats and for quick energy; if you choose to use candies, add them as extras to an already nutritious diet.

NON-CHOCOLATE PRODUCTS
Sesame-honey candies, caramels, jelly beans, yogurt-covered candies, fruit or nuts, etc.

FLAVORED BAKING CHIPS and CAROB CHIPS
Semi-sweet and milk chocolate, chocolate mint, butterscotch, and peanut butter; good for trail food, baking, and adding to hot cereal with nuts.

DESSERTS (instant type—add water only)
BROWNIE MIX and GINGERBREAD MIX
   Both can be "scrambled" instead of baked, or added to pancake batter for gingerbread or chocolate pancakes.

CHEESECAKE MIX
   A wonderfully creative dessert topped with wild berries; Grapenuts or granola make good crusts.

PUDDING MIX
   Variety of flavors; quick and easy; good source of carbohydrates; good plain or as a pie or cake filling.

JELLO
   Variety of flavors; makes an excellent hot drink.

BASES, SOUPS, AND SAUCES
BEEF and CHICKEN BASE
   Comes in bulk, packets or cubes; good for soup, hot drinks, gravies, and sauces; very salty—use sparingly and taste dish before using additional salt; for added flavor add to cooking water for grains, pastas, and so on.

hold the salt!

MISO
   A natural base made from soybeans, rice, or barley that is very good for the digestive system; add to already cooked foods as boiling kills its healthy active enzymes.

VEGETABLE BOUILLON CUBES or PACKETS
   Use the same as beef or chicken bases; vegetarian; makes a good hot drink.

TOMATO POWDER
   Very popular and versatile; good in soups and pizza, spaghetti or Mexican sauces.

CHEESE POWDER
   Lightweight substitute for real cheese, especially in soups and sprinkled on popcorn; handy for extended trips to lengthen the cheese ration since it doesn't spoil.

SOUR CREAM POWDER
Great with curry or Mexican dishes or as a dessert topping; tasty, but bulk is difficult to find.

ASSORTED SAUCE MIXES
Available in grocery and natural food stores in individual packets in many different flavors—pesto, vinaigrette, taco, sour cream, and more. Read cooking instructions carefully before choosing.

CUP-OF-SOUP
Popular and versatile; can be used as a soup or flavoring base.

RAMEN SOUP
Tasty, quick, high carbohydrate meal.

BREAKFAST FOODS

GRANOLA
Buy commercially or make your own from oatmeal; great as breakfast or trail food.

GRAPENUTS
Versatile; good for breakfast or use as a pie crust, sprinkle over the top of casseroles, add to muffin or pancake batter.

KELLOGG'S CRACKLIN' OAT BRAN
Versatile as trail food or with hot or cold milk for breakfast; affectionately known as "puppy chow;" good source of fiber.

OATMEAL, WHEAT, RICE, and RYE CEREALS
Regular and instant types are available in bulk or individual packets; instant cereals are most versatile and cook more quickly; leftovers make great breads.

HOMINY GRITS
Regular or instant types are available in bulk or individual packets; a corn product that is fast, easy, and versatile; good as a hot cereal, side-dish, or in casseroles.

DEHYDRATED SLICED POTATOES
Great if hydrated completely—hot water is a *must*; resemble home fries when seasoned and fried.

DEHYDRATED HASH BROWNS
Rehydrate about 15 minutes in hot water, drain, and fry; good with spices and cheeses; make great potato pancakes.

PANCAKE MIX
Buy commercially or make your own; quick and versatile; leftover pancakes are good with spreadables as a trail food.

DINNER FOODS

PASTAS
Includes macaroni, spaghetti, and various noodles such as egg, alphabet, ramen type, lasagne, etc.; make quick, easy, versatile meals; great variety of colors, flavors, and shapes are available; whole grain types take same cooking time as white pastas but are slightly chewy when done and if over-cooked they become pasty and cement-like; good source of carbohydrates.

GRAINS

Hint: If you're going to be at high altitudes, a pressure cooker can be invaluable for cooking these foods.

WHITE RICE
Available in many forms; each variety differs in taste and cooking time; choose type carefully where time and fuel are factors; very versatile for dinner, breakfast or dessert; high in carbohydrates; forms a complete protein combination with milk, cheese, sesame seeds, wheat, or seeds and nuts.

BROWN RICE
Same as above but in a more natural form; best if presoaked or cooked in a pressure cooker as it takes a long time to cook at altitude.

BULGAR or BULGAR SOY GRITS and COUS-COUS
Both are wheat products that cook quickly and can be used for breakfast, dinner, or baking.

MILLET and BARLEY
These grains take considerable prep time; need to be presoaked or pressure cooked at altitude; great combined with beans or legumes to make a complete protein.

FALAFEL
A Middle Eastern staple made from ground chick-peas, yellow split peas, and spices; very spicy flavor; interesting change of pace for dinner or cooked up in patties as a trail food.

BEANS AND LEGUMES

PINTO BEANS, BLACK-EYED PEAS, NAVY BEANS, BLACK BEANS, LENTILS

These beans and legumes are very good but take considerable time to prepare, especially at high altitudes; even fast cooking types take more than half an hour to cook so are best presoaked or pressure cooked; a complete protein when combined with grains, cheese, or seeds; pinto beans are a staple for many Mexican dishes; black-eyed peas are great with ham, bacon, or grains; lentils are good in soups or stews or can be sprouted for a salad.

REFRIED BEAN POWDER
A new product; tasty and quick; good spread on tortillas with cheese and picante.

POTATOES
INSTANT, PEARL, FLAKED
Fast, easy, tasty, and versatile; good source of carbohydrates; good in potato pancakes or as thickener for soups; great as a one-cup meal when combined with a Cup-of-Soup packet, cheese, and/or diced ham.

LOW MOISTURE/DRIED VEGETABLES
PEAS, CARROTS, RED and GREEN BELL PEPPER FLAKES, MIXED VEGETABLES, DRIED ONIONS, FREEZE-DRIED VEGETABLE SALAD MIX, PARSLEY
Very popular because they add color, flavor, and texture to meals; must be added to cooking water before it starts to boil so that they are rehydrated by serving time; proper rehydration prevents the stomach cramps and gas often associated with dried foods.

CHEESE
CHEDDAR, JACK, SWISS, MOZZARELLA, CREAM CHEESE, PARMESAN, ETC.
A good source of protein and fats that is flavorful and versatile; real cheese is worth the extra trouble, but care should be taken in packaging to avoid mold on long trips (dipping cheese in wax helps); lower fat and hard cheeses hold up better; cut in 1/4 to 1/2 inch cubes for easier use in winter. In choosing your cheese, pick one that is versatile with a taste that you won't tire of soon.

MEATS—COLD WEATHER
HAM, PRECOOKED
Flavorful; good source of fats and protein; easier to use when precut in small cubes since it cooks faster and small amounts can be broken off when needed; great in pastas, soups, and beans.

BACON and SAUSAGE LINKS
Flavorful addition to casseroles and one-pot meals; good source of fats and protein; cut bacon in smaller pieces for ease of use; drippings are useful for sauces, gravies, etc.

HAMBURGER
Good protein source; less fatty than pork products; good cooked as patties for bagel burgers or crumbled and cooked as an ingredient in casseroles and tomato sauces. Hamburger can also be browned at home and then frozen. At camp add to casseroles or make tacos.

MEATS—WARM WEATHER

BEEF JERKY, SUMMER SAUSAGE, BACON and HAM "BITS"
Spicy, tasty, and chewy; great as trail food or added to summer meals; do not require refrigeration.

CANNED MEATS
Small cans of chicken, turkey, and tuna are an excellent lightweight source of protein to combine with rice or noodles for all kinds of casseroles.

PRECOOKED HAMBURGER GRANULES
These are available at backpacking stores. They are completely unseasoned (not even salt) and are very versatile.

FLOUR, BAKING GOODS, AND SWEETENERS

BAKING MIX
Either commercial or home-made (see recipe index); fast, easy, and convenient for quick meals; great for pancakes, biscuits, dumplings, muffins, coffee cake, and pizza crust.

WHITE and WHOLE WHEAT FLOURS
Use for baking and thickeners; whole wheat is more nutritious but heavier; white is better for making white sauces and lighter breads and cakes.

SPECIALTY FLOURS
Soy, rye, buckwheat, and graham flours are very nutritious and good in breads, but are more costly, more difficult to use, and become rancid more quickly due to their higher fat content.

CORNMEAL
Used to make tortillas, chappaties, cookies, polenta (hot cereal), and for breading fish.

WHEAT GERM, BRAN FLAKES
Great supplements to boost nutritional value of meals; wheat germ is a protein source; bran provides fiber.

BROWN SUGAR
Use in baking, hot cereals, drinks, candies; mix with vinegar for sweet-sour dishes; better flavor and texture than refined white sugar.

HONEY, SYRUP
Good source of carbohydrates for quick energy; use as a spreadable, in baking, or on hot cereals.

BEVERAGES

TEA and COFFEE
Use a variety of teas. Coffee substitutes without caffeine are available in freeze-dried forms, but some people prefer the ritual of making coffee from grounds. Coffee and teas are diuretics, and it is important, especially at high altitudes, that you do not become dehydrated, so use in moderation.

INSTANT COCOA
Good, popular hot drink; goes further if extended with powdered milk; can be added to cakes, cookies, frostings, and puddings for a chocolate flavor.

POWDERED MILK
Several powdered forms of milk are available: instant whole milk, instant non-fat milk, non-instant whole milk, and buttermilk. Whole milk has more calories and vitamin A; instant powders dissolve best in cold water and can then be heated. Non-instant powders are good for cooking and are more compact, but are harder to mix properly. Buttermilk powder is excellent for cooking but less popular for drinking. Add powdered milk to beverages, casseroles and baked goods to enhance flavor and nutritional value; good source of protein and calcium. Breakfast drinks based on milk come in a variety of flavors and can be bought in most supermarkets.

APPLE CIDER MIX
Good hot or cold; great as a sweetener in tea or hot cereals; good added to stewed fruits or dessert cooking water.

FRUIT CRYSTALS (TANG, KOOL-AID, ETC.)
Add flavor to treated water; good source of carbohydrates and vitamin C; mix with snow to make snow cones.

MISCELLANEOUS

MARGARINE

Good source of fats and flavoring; necessary in making any sauce; helps retain moisture in cooked grain products; less expensive than butter, and unlike butter it can keep without refrigeration; unwrap and carry in plastic bags or plastic jars; repeated freezing and thawing will change texture, but it will still be usable. Liquid margarine is easy to pack and use but should be double-bagged for safety.

POWDERED EGGS

Whole egg powder is best if used quickly; good in baked items, casseroles, and omelets.

NON-FOOD ITEMS

Add toilet paper, matches, fuel bottles, and soap to your ration list so these important items are not forgotten. Use white toilet paper and biodegradable soap. Pack soap with other toilet articles and not with the food.

THE SPICE KIT

Spice and Herb Identification

Hint: Remember that not everyone feels the same way about chili powder or curry that you do. Keep your tentmates in mind when seasoning foods.

A short explanation of commonly used spices for the beginning cook:

Powders

Salt	White granules. Use with care as over salting can ruin a meal. Since most bases are heavily salted, the use of this seasoning in conjunction with a base is unnecessary. But if a meal tastes flat, it probably needs salt.
Black Pepper	Black and white granules. Enhances most main dishes. Tends to be a little hot.

Garlic Powder	Light yellowish-white granules. Very popular seasoning. Adds flavor to main dishes, breads, soups, and sauces. A must for Italian dishes!
Chili Powder	Dark red granules. Tends to be a little hot and spicy. Mostly used in Mexican type meals such as chili, burritos and quesadillas.
Curry	Bright yellowish-brown color, which is imparted to the food. Used frequently in Middle Eastern dishes. Can be quite hot and spicy. Often complemented by fruits such as raisins, apricots, coconut, and pineapple.
Cinnamon	Fine brown powder with a sweet smell. Used in sweet breads and desserts. Complements hot milk, cocoa, and hot cereals.
Spike	Greenish-brown color with specks of yellow. A combination of different vegetables and herbs used as a natural seasoning. Its lemon/salt flavor appeals to many different palates. Great in cheesy type casseroles or sprinkled on tortillas.
Oregano*	Light green chopped leaves. Used frequently in Italian tomato sauces and as a garnish for casseroles. Has a pungent aroma.
Basil*	Dark green chopped leaves that smell like licorice. Commonly used in tomato or white sauces.
Baking Powder	Dense white powder used as a quick leavening agent.
Baking Yeast	Beige granules used in conjunction with sugar and water to help raise flour for breads, rolls, pizza, etc.

* Small amounts of these spices should be put in your hand and crushed to release spice's flavor.

Cumin Powder	Dense greenish-brown powder with a pungent woody aroma. Used frequently in rice or Mexican bean dishes, often with chili or curry powder.
Powdered Mustard	Light yellow powder used to add tang to white sauces or in grain and cheese casseroles. Has a sharp, hot flavor.
Dill Weed	Green flower heads. Excellent in soups, breads, or muffins. Very aromatic!
Apple Pie Spice	A combination of cinnamon, nutmeg, allspice, and cardamom. Brown powder with tart sweet aroma used in sweet breads, desserts, fruit stews, pies, and hot beverages.
Cayenne	Bright red powder that is very hot and spicy. Used in sauces or as a condiment.

Liquids

Oil	Use for sauteing vegetables, popping popcorn, or oil and vinegar dressing. Also used as an ingredient in baked goods.
Vinegar	A tangy, colorless liquid used in salad dressings, sweet and sours and picante sauce.
Soy Sauce	Salty, dark liquid made from soybeans. Good over grains or in white sauces. Often used as a salt substitute.
Vanilla	Sweet smelling dark liquid used in sweet baked goods, desserts, hot cereals, and hot drinks.
Tabasco/Hot Sauce	Bright red liquid made from hot red chile peppers. Used as a condiment over grains, pastas and in soups. A preferred spice for the hot palate.

PACKAGING

The first thing you will want to do once you have assembled all of your food is to repackage it. Cardboard, paper, foil, and cans are all excess weight and potential litter.

At NOLS we use two-ply plastic bags to package almost all our food. We purchase commercial bags that can be lightly tied in a knot. Plastic bags are lightweight, reusable, and allow you to see what's inside. Use a permanent marker to identify contents if you're packing your own food.

We use small plastic bottles with screw on lids for spices and wide-mouth Nalgene containers for honey, peanut butter, and margarine.

Other possible food containers include Ziploc bags, freezer bags, Seal-A-Meal bags, Tupperware, and squeeze tubes.

If you are using a meal planning system you may want to package each day's meals together, or pack breakfasts, lunches, and dinners together by meal type. Label with indelible ink and include recipe instructions.

Always be very careful when packaging food to avoid any chance of contamination by soap, stove fuel, or a leaking lighter. In packing your pack, try to keep your food above these items. Heavy items like food should generally be high and close to your body unless you'll be hiking through boulder fields or deadfall. Then carry your weight lower for better balance when jumping or twisting.

THE SPICE KIT

Where to Pack Weight in Your Pack

TRAIL HIKING :
PACK HEAVY ITEMS HIGH AND
CLOSE TO THE BODY

HIKING THROUGH BOULDER
FIELDS or DEAD FALL :
CARRY WEIGHT LOWER TO GIVE
YOU BETTER BALANCE FOR
JUMPING AND TWISTING.

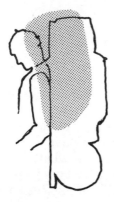

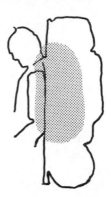

WHERE FOOD IS LOCATED
IN YOUR PACK :

FOOD, COOKING
EQUIPMENT AND
OTHER HEAVY
ITEMS.

MAKE SURE THAT POSSIBLE
CONTAMINANTS SUCH AS
STOVE FUEL, LIGHTERS, AND
SOAP ARE CARRIED BELOW
FOOD.

RATION RESUPPLY

At NOLS each student carries his/her share of the rations inside a 22" nylon-zippered duffle bag. We find that a ten-day food supply (15-20 lbs.) is the maximum that most people can carry. For longer trips you will want to plan a re-supply.

There are a number of ways to re-supply your expedition:

Roadhead Re-supply

Either make a loop returning to your car, have a second car, or arrange for a friend to meet you with a prepackaged ration at a roadhead.

Commercial Packers

Commercial packers will deliver rations to a predetermined point at a predetermined time. Price, weight limits, and packaging requirements vary with individual packers. A horse can generally carry a 150 lb. load.

Pack Animals

Backpacking with burros, horses, llamas, or even goats is an option. Most public lands require special grazing permits for pack animals. You should have experience handling these animals. A good method for horsepackers is to box plastic bags of food in cardboard boxes with even poundages in each box (we use 25 pounds).

Mailing

Mail yourself packaged re-rations care of General Delivery to a post office in a town near your route. Be sure to include a "to be picked up by" date.

Boats

If you are near navigable waterways, consider resupply by motorboat or canoe.

Caches

These are illegal in most National Parks and designated Wilderness and Primitive Areas. But if permission is obtained, packaging is important. For caches, food should be put in waterproof, animal-proof containers. Cache only predetermined amounts of food so nothing will be left over. After using, completely clean up the cache site and camouflage any evidence a cache was ever there.

Air Drop

Air drops are also illegal in many ares. Check with local authorities and your pilot first. Food for an air drop needs to be packaged so bags won't burst on impact. For air drops, double box food in cardboard boxes, pack very tightly and reinforce with strapping tape. Be sure the box will fit out the airplane window.

Regardless of how you choose to re-ration, a few guidelines must be followed. Have all information concerning where and when, in writing, with duplicates for you and your re-supplier. Preferably have locations written on accurate topographic maps. Make arrangements with the re-supplier concerning what will happen if you do not get to the re-supply point on time and have this information in writing also. Be sure to check references if you are hiring a re-supplier.

Food for re-rationing should be bagged in plastic bags. Have food already packaged for the re-supplier—bagged, boxed, weighed, and labelled as applicable.

Do not depend on the re-supplier to do your shopping and packaging. Be sure the re-supply point is completely cleaned up when you leave.

Hint: For any type of re-supply, pack food so that a loss of any one box will not mean the loss of any one type of food. Pack matches in several places as they can ignite by rubbing against each other and leave you "Matchless."

COOKING

EQUIPMENT AND STOVES • COOKING ON FIRES
ENVIRONMENTAL CONSIDERATIONS
COOKING HINTS FOR BEGINNERS

EQUIPMENT
AND STOVES

At NOLS we have learned to produce gourmet meals with a bare minimum of cooking utensils. Each student has his/her own bowl, a NOLS mug (insulated 12-ounce cup with a lid), and a spoon. Each cook group is issued 2 (3-quart) stainless steel pots, 1 non-stick or Silverstone 12" fry pan with flat lid and no plastic parts, 1 plastic spatula, 1 large plastic spoon, 1 pocketknife, 1 collapsible 2 1/2-gallon water jug, cotton gloves, and potgrips.

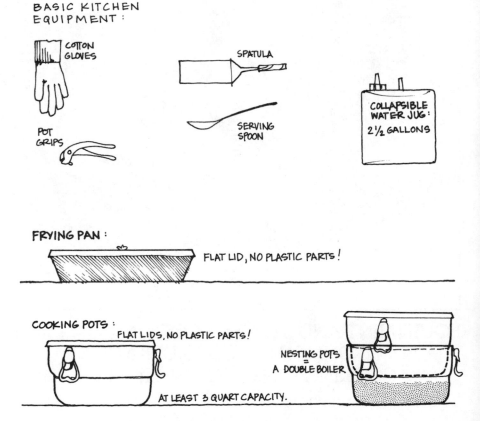

BASIC KITCHEN EQUIPMENT:

COTTON GLOVES

SPATULA

POT GRIPS

SERVING SPOON

COLLAPSIBLE WATER JUG: 2½ GALLONS

FRYING PAN:

FLAT LID, NO PLASTIC PARTS!

COOKING POTS:

FLAT LIDS, NO PLASTIC PARTS!

NESTING POTS = A DOUBLE BOILER

AT LEAST 3 QUART CAPACITY.

OPTIONAL ITEMS :

SMALL
GRATER

SMALL
WHISK

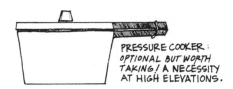

PRESSURE COOKER :
OPTIONAL BUT WORTH
TAKING! A NECESSITY
AT HIGH ELEVATIONS.

Optional luxuries include a small cheese grater, small whisk for blending sauces, a folding grate, and a pressure cooker. Backpacking pressure cookers are not currently being manufactured. Some people are packing the smaller aluminum pressure cookers available from hardware stores. They are heavy to pack but can't be beat for cooking beans and legumes quickly, especially at high altitudes.

There are a number of excellent backpacking stoves on the market today. The most practical ones use white gas. However, white gas (Coleman fuel) is not always available in foreign countries. If this is a concern, interchangeable parts are available for some stoves that allow you to use kerosene. At NOLS we use mainly Optimus 111 Hikers, which, although they are heavy, stand up well to the hard and extended use of NOLS courses. The Coleman Peak I is a relatively inexpensive lightweight alternative. MSR makes excellent lightweight stoves, but they are rather delicate for institutional use.

Have a clear understanding of how your stove works and carry the parts and tools necessary to repair it in an emergency. Keep it clean and dry and clean the orifice after each use.

Locate your stove on a level surface protected from the wind and away from any vegetation. If possible, position the stove with pressure release cap directed away from your face but with on/off valve accessible. Keep the area clear of all burnable materials.

Store fuel in fuel bottles and use funnels or pouring spouts to fill your stove. Fill stoves away from your cooking area and any open flames. Stoves should be filled after each use once they're cool. You never know when you'll have to start one in a hurry.

Figuring fuel amounts:

During the summer expect to use 1/2 quart bottle per stove, per day (based on a 3 person cook group).

Example: $\dfrac{7 \text{ stoves x } 8 \text{ days} = 56}{2}$ = 28 quarts (= 7 gallons)

SUMMER

Or figure on 1/6 quart per person per day.

$\dfrac{20 \text{ people x } 8 \text{ days} = 160 \text{ man days}}{6}$ = 26.66 (= about 7 gallons)

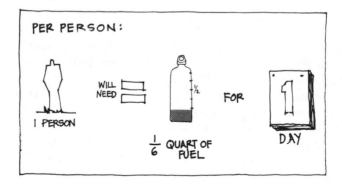

During the winter, if you'll be melting snow for water or if you'll be at altitudes of over 10,000 feet, plan on 1 bottle per stove per day, then round up to the next highest gallon (based on a 3 person cook group or 1 gallon per person every 10 days).

WINTER : IF YOU PLAN ON MELTING SNOW FOR WATER

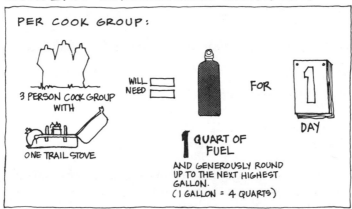

PER COOK GROUP:

3 PERSON COOK GROUP WITH

ONE TRAIL STOVE

WILL NEED

1 QUART OF FUEL

FOR

1 DAY

AND GENEROUSLY ROUND UP TO THE NEXT HIGHEST GALLON.
(1 GALLON = 4 QUARTS)

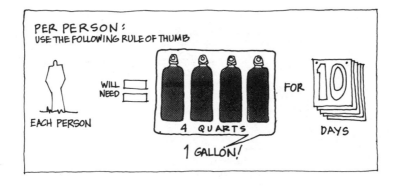

PER PERSON:
USE THE FOLLOWING RULE OF THUMB

EACH PERSON

WILL NEED

4 QUARTS

1 GALLON!

FOR

10 DAYS

COOKING ON FIRES

Appropriate backcountry campfire sites have five qualities:

1. They are safe.
2. They minimize damage to the environment.
3. Building the fire is simple.
4. Firewood is abundant.
5. They are easy to clean and camouflage.

For safety's sake, always build campfires far away from dry grass, trees, branches, and root systems; never leave a fire unattended; and know and respect the fire restrictions of the area.

THE PROPERLY SET UP KITCHEN:

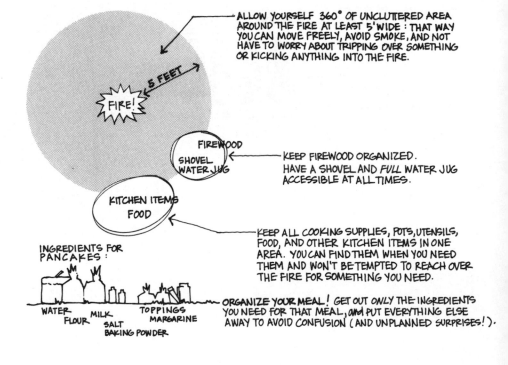

ALLOW YOURSELF 360° OF UNCLUTTERED AREA AROUND THE FIRE AT LEAST 5' WIDE : THAT WAY YOU CAN MOVE FREELY, AVOID SMOKE, AND NOT HAVE TO WORRY ABOUT TRIPPING OVER SOMETHING OR KICKING ANYTHING INTO THE FIRE.

5 FEET

FIRE!

FIREWOOD
SHOVEL
WATER JUG

KEEP FIREWOOD ORGANIZED. HAVE A SHOVEL AND *FULL* WATER JUG ACCESSIBLE AT ALL TIMES.

KITCHEN ITEMS
FOOD

KEEP ALL COOKING SUPPLIES, POTS, UTENSILS, FOOD, AND OTHER KITCHEN ITEMS IN ONE AREA. YOU CAN FIND THEM WHEN YOU NEED THEM AND WON'T BE TEMPTED TO REACH OVER THE FIRE FOR SOMETHING YOU NEED.

INGREDIENTS FOR PANCAKES:

WATER
FLOUR MILK
SALT
BAKING POWDER
TOPPINGS
MARGARINE

ORGANIZE YOUR MEAL! GET OUT ONLY THE INGREDIENTS YOU NEED FOR THAT MEAL, and PUT EVERYTHING ELSE AWAY TO AVOID CONFUSION (AND UNPLANNED SURPRISES!).

In a degraded area, the best site for a fire is in an existing fire ring. In a pristine area, first ask yourself if a fire is necessary. If so, build a mound fire, pile up mineral soil several inches thick on a flat rocky surface or fire pan/cloth. Where do you find mineral soil? Uprooted trees, sandy areas near streambeds, or exposed soil near boulder areas are all excellent sources.

For a pit fire, simply scrape a shallow pit several inches deep and build your fire in this depression. Never build a fire pit in vegetation. Severe depressions will still be evident years later. The secret to avoiding environmental damage is to dig your fire pit in exposed mineral soil.

MOUND FIRE :

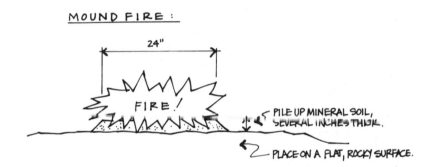

FIRE!

PILE UP MINERAL SOIL, SEVERAL INCHES THICK.

PLACE ON A FLAT, ROCKY SURFACE.

FIRE PIT:

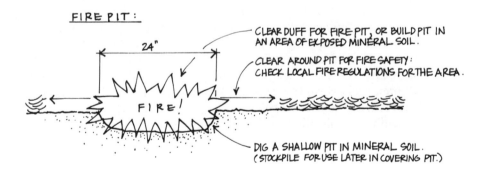

CLEAR DUFF FOR FIRE PIT, OR BUILD PIT IN AN AREA OF EXPOSED MINERAL SOIL.

CLEAR AROUND PIT FOR FIRE SAFETY: CHECK LOCAL FIRE REGULATIONS FOR THE AREA.

FIRE!

DIG A SHALLOW PIT IN MINERAL SOIL. (STOCKPILE FOR USE LATER IN COVERING PIT.)

The best firewood is small diameter (1-2 inches) lying loose on the ground and *not* attached to downed timber to preserve pristine wilderness. Small pieces of wood are easier to burn to ash and are less critical to the ecosystem. Try to collect wood from a wide area: do not denude the immediate surroundings. Collect only enough for a small fire.

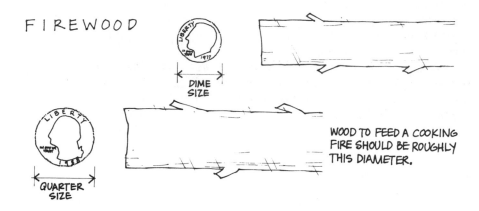

FIREWOOD

DIME
SIZE

QUARTER
SIZE

WOOD TO FEED A COOKING
FIRE SHOULD BE ROUGHLY
THIS DIAMETER.

Be sure to allow yourself enough time for thorough clean up and camouflaging of the site. Leave your campsite as clean as you found it (or cleaner) for the benefit of future campers. Regardless of whether you used an established fire ring or constructed a fire in a pristine area, burn any remaining partially burned wood to ash at least 30 minutes before disposing of your fire signs. Crush any remaining charcoal. If you can sift your fingers through this ash and powder, your fire is out. Scatter the remains and any leftover firewood far from the site.

If you constructed a mound fire, after scattering the leftover ash and charcoal, return the soil to where you originally found it; if the mound was built on a rock, rinse the rock off. When using a pit, after dispersing the ash, fill it with excavated soil. Finally, camouflage the area to match the surroundings. This allows others to enjoy the same site later.

Baking:

You can use coals from your campfire to create a backcountry dutch oven for baking. Set your bake pan on a flat bed of coals and shovel coals on the top in an *even* layer (for even cooking) on the lid. The coals should feel very hot but not quite burn when you hold your hand six inches away for 8 seconds. Cool by spreading or sprinkling with sand. The coals on the top should be hotter than those on the bottom. Replenish coals as they go dead.

BAKING WITH FIRES AND STOVES :

SOURCES OF TOP HEAT! → TWIGGY FIRES OR COALS

SOURCES OF BOTTOM HEAT! → CAN BE COALS OR STOVE

SOURCES OF TOP HEAT :

WILL FEEL VERY HOT BUT SHOULD NOT BURN WHEN YOU HOLD YOUR HAND 6" AWAY.

HEAT!

BUILD A SMALL TWIGGY FIRE OR SHOVEL COALS FROM THE FIRE ON TO THE LID OF THE PAN.

SOURCES OF BOTTOM HEAT :

"ROUND THE CLOCK"

BAKING ON A STOVE : THINK OF THE PAN AS A CLOCK FACE. PLACE THE PAN OVER THE STOVE FLAME OFF CENTER TOWARDS 12 O'CLOCK, AND HOLD FOR A FEW MINUTES. CONTINUE CLOCKWISE, HEATING EACH 1/3 OF THE PAN EACH TIME.

TOP VIEW:

STEP 1 HOT!

STEP 2 HOT!

STEP 3 HOT!

GO AROUND AS MANY TIMES AS NEEDED TO BAKE THE CONTENTS.

BAKING ON COALS : USE THE SAME TECHNIQUE, MOVING THE PAN EVERY FEW MINUTES.

Be very careful when you check progress. It's safest to scrape all the coals off the lid before you peek. Don't peek too soon or your cake might fall. Wait at least 10 minutes unless you smell burning. And always wear an expendable pair of gloves, or better yet a pair of oven mitts, when baking over an open fire.

It is also possible to bake on your stove. Use a low flame under your bake pan and build a small fire with twigs on the lid of your bake pan. This is called a "twiggy" fire. In order for this method to work, you need a bake pan like the one described in the equipment section.

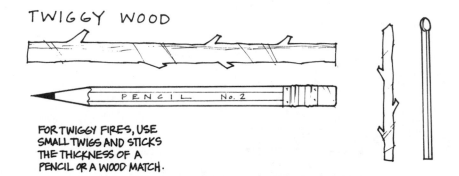

TWIGGY WOOD

FOR TWIGGY FIRES, USE SMALL TWIGS AND STICKS THE THICKNESS OF A PENCIL OR A WOOD MATCH.

Other baking tips:

- Fill your pan only half full since baked goods rise.
- Pan should never be filled to the point ingredients touch the lid or they'll burn.
- Rotate your pan every few minutes to ensure even baking. This is called the "Round the Clock Method."
- If you're above tree line where no firewood is available, some items like biscuits and brownies can be cooked without a twiggy fire by cooking on one side and then flipping them. Make a very stiff dough to start.
- You can use an ensolite pad for rolling dough. Improvise a rolling pin from a water bottle or a fishing pole case wrapped in plastic bags.

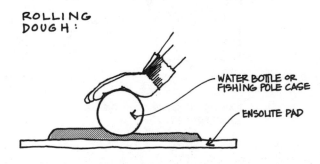

ROLLING DOUGH:

WATER BOTTLE OR FISHING POLE CASE

ENSOLITE PAD

ENVIRONMENTAL CONSIDERATIONS

Kitchen Clean-up

The basic rule of kitchen clean-up is: pack out what you pack in. By repackaging your food, you've already eliminated most potential litter and minimized you pack-out load. With proper meal planning and careful cooking (no burning!) you can also eliminate most leftovers. But if you do end up with extra cooked food, use it at another meal or pack it out.

Scattering food is unsightly and attracts scavengers. One exception is fish remains. Disperse them widely out of sight and well away from campsites. Don't throw remains into high alpine lakes and streams—they won't decompose in the cold water.

Water used for cooking and dishwashing should be scattered widely, at least 200 feet away from any water source and far away from any campsites. Remember to separate food scraps first and pack them out. NOLS recommends this method over sump holes which attract insects and are frequently dug up by animals. Burning leftovers successfully requires an exceptionally hot fire and usually results in a mess.

NATURAL SCRUBRUSHES :

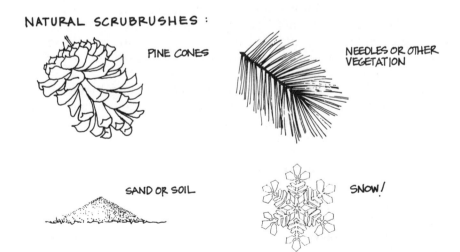

PINE CONES

NEEDLES OR OTHER VEGETATION

SAND OR SOIL

SNOW!

At NOLS, we use soap only for washing hands before food preparation. We clean the dishes with nature's scrub brushes—sand, pinecones, pine needles, and bunches of grass—and give them a good rinse with boiling water just prior to eating. This method eliminates adding soapy dishwater to the environment and also avoids tummy upsets caused by soap residues on the dishes. However, if you want to use soap, carrying a small bottle of dishwashing detergent and using a few drops for cleaning works well.

Water Safety

These days, no matter how remote the area, there's a good chance the water supply is contaminated by *Giardia lamblia*, a parasitic microorganism that can make life miserable. Symptoms don't appear for two to three weeks after ingestion, but include severe nausea, vomiting, diarrhea, and loss of fluids.

The only *sure* way to avoid contamination is to boil all drinking water 3-5 minutes (boil longer at high altitude). Since this isn't always practical, most people either use a filter or treat their water with iodine. If you do use a filter, be sure the filter's pore size is no larger than 0.4 microns to assure protection against *Giardia*.

Bear Country

When traveling in bear country, be sure to check recommended bear practices for your area. You'll need to take extra precautions in the selection of your kitchen site. The cooking areas should be at least a hundred yards distant from the sleeping area. Be sure to empty your pack of all food and odorous substances, including trail food, soap, and toothpaste, and store them in the kitchen area. Be extra careful to avoid spills on your clothing. Fish and other greasy food smells are especially attractive to bears, so take precautions to minimize personal contact with these substances.

At night all food should be hung. If you are camping at tree level, hang food so it's at least 12 feet above ground at its lowest point and hanging at least four feet from any part of the tree. Choose a location at least a hundred yards from your sleeping area.

Cold Weather Considerations

It takes 15-20 minutes to melt snow and another 10-15 minutes to boil the water—a half hour before cooking can even begin! Therefore most food in the winter should be easy to prepare and of the one-pot meal variety. Cut foods like cheese, salami and bacon into bite size pieces before your trip. Once they freeze, they become so hard to dice you may cut yourself instead.

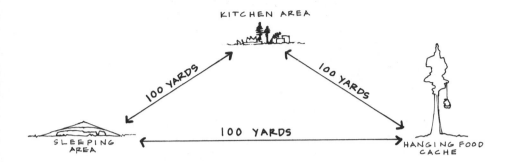

KITCHEN AREA

100 YARDS

100 YARDS

100 YARDS

SLEEPING AREA

HANGING FOOD CACHE

MAKE SURE TO EMPTY YOUR PACK OF ALL FOOD AND ODOROUS SUBSTANCES, INCLUDING TRAIL FOOD, SOAP, AND TOOTHPASTE.

Obtaining water by melting snow becomes a major task in the winter. You have to keep at it all the time, or you'll fall behind. It's easy to scorch a snow-filled pot if it's set directly on a high flame. To avoid scorching, add a little water to the bottom of the pot.

Another method, if spending a sunny day in camp, is to put a dark colored plastic tarp or rain parka in a hollow in the snow. When you place a small amount of snow at a tie in the tarp, the sun's energy absorbed by the dark color will melt the snow. Large amounts of water can be obtained this way.

Because liquid intake is so important in winter (everyone should consume 3-4 quarts per day), bring along extra soup bases and drink mixes. Coffee and tea are diuretics, so use in moderation in the winter. Also, it's wise to take a full water bottle with you when you go to bed. It makes a nice hot water bottle and wrapping it in a piece of ensolite will help insulate it.

High Altitude

Since the time needed to boil water doubles for each 5,000-foot increase in elevation, a 10-minute meal at sea level requires 40 minutes at 10,000 feet. As in winter, you'll want to prepare simple one-pot meals that require little preparation or clean-up. Carbohydrates are more appealing and more easily digested than proteins or fats at high altitudes. Lighter meals are encouraged during the first three days of acclimatization, continuing with small frequent feedings during the entire duration at altitude.

Fluid intake is more important than ever and should be monitored closely. Dehydration can cause acute discomfort and affect physical performance. Aim for 3-5 quarts per day.

COOKING HINTS
FOR BEGINNERS

"What is it, and how do I cook it quickly?" is the most common question students ask their instructors on NOLS Courses. Listed below are some of the most common pitfalls for beginning cooks.

What is it?

At NOLS, with thousands of bags of food bagged daily, we don't mark the contents. If you're in doubt, stick your finger in the food bag and taste its contents. This will help to avoid mistakes like pouring cheesecake into macaroni or pouring potato pearls into cocoa, thinking you're adding milk. These mistakes are common and can ruin your meal.

After the first few days when you become more familiar with your rations, it becomes easy to identify foods by the way they look and feel. Powdered milk tastes sweet and it squeaks when you squeeze the bag; flour tastes like paste and squishes to the touch; cheesecake squeaks and is very aromatic. Potato pearls squeak, taste salty and smell like butter. It is the white items like milk, cheesecake, flour, potato pearls, etc. that will get you into trouble, so remember to taste before you mix!

How do I cook it?

Use the stoves carefully so as not to burn your meals. The lightweight cook pots we issue are very thin on the bottom and transmit heat quite rapidly. It is imperative that you sit and monitor your cooking meal at all times. Just two minutes on high heat is all it takes to burn a meal. Keep in mind that no matter how much you season a burned meal, it still tastes burned!

A general rule is to bring your water to a boil, add your contents and stir. Turn heat on low, cover and simmer, checking frequently by sticking a spoon down the middle of your contents to see the bottom of the pan. Usually if you smell something burning, it's too late.

How do I know how much seasoning to use?

Seasoning is largely a matter of taste, not an exact science. Some guidelines:
- Never pour seasoning directly in the pot. Pour into the palm of your hand first.
- Start with a little, taste, and add some more.

- Take into account the fact that the flavor will intensify with cooking. After seasoning, allow food to cook about 10 minutes and taste again before adding more.
- Another option is to have your tentmates season their own portions to taste.

How much should I make?
On average, a recipe requiring 1 pound of dry food (pasta, grain, beans, etc.) feeds three people, depending on individual appetites and what else is on the menu.

What else should I know?
- Always start with a clean pot to avoid burning old food stuck on the bottom.
- A bland "soapy" taste is most often due to lack of salt. Salt brings out the flavor in everything, but don't overdo it. Taste first—the flavor bases already have a lot of salt in them.
- Overcooking is usually caused by poor timing of multiple ingredients. Add freeze-dried food to cold water, boil 10 to 15 minutes, then add rice or pasta. Thickeners (flour, potato pearls, milk, cheese) should be added just before the dish is done to avoid scorching.
- Another way to avoid burning foods, especially eggs or cheese sauce, is to use your pots like a double boiler: put one pot on the stove with a few inches of boiling water and set the other pot inside it.
- Plan ahead: If you're cook of the day, start planning dinner early in the day while you're on the trail. Have a mental agenda of what needs to be done.
- When you get to camp, boil water for hot drinks while you assemble ingredients. Assign food prep tasks to your tentmates. Use your time and fuel efficiently.
- Tired, cold, and hungry cooks are the most likely to make mistakes. (And tired, cold and hungry tentmates are the least forgiving.)

What if I have too much?

Hint: Towards the end of a ration period, you might want to get together with other cook groups to re-pool and re-distribute your leftover food for a fresh start.

If you have lots of	Then
Dried fruit and nuts	Chop them and add to hot cereals, pancakes, cookies, cakes, rice dishes.
Dates	See Stuffed Dates and Fruit Bar recipes.
Beef, chicken or vegetable bases	Add them to cooking water for rice, cous-cous, bulgar and pasta; make gravies; add to boiling water for a quick hot drink.
Potato Pearls	Try making potato and cheese patties.
Bulgar	Add it to macaroni or rice to stretch them; try Spanish Bulgar recipe or Tabouleh Salad or add leftovers to Leftover Bread recipe.
Oatmeal	Make granola, oatmeal bread, cookies, or cake; use as topping for Apple Crisp; use in Oat Stones recipe or for dumplings; try the No-Bake Cookies and You'll Never Believe It Soup.
Raw sunflower seeds	Add to baked goods, granola, hot cereal, casseroles, or try dry-roasting them and sprinkling with hot sauce or cayenne.
Cheese	Fry thin slices in an oiled pan; make Cheese Bombs or Cheese Carumba; serve with Oat Stones as a trail food; crumble into soups, potatoes, pastas; make Nachos.
Miso	Add to boiling water for a hot drink good for digestion problems; make Bulgar-Miso Sauce or Peanut-Miso Sauce.

Flour	See baking and dessert recipes (many do not require twiggy fires); make pancakes, biscuits, dumplings, tortillas.
Cornmeal	Make polenta, corn tortillas, mixed grain balls, cornmeal cookies, cornmeal pancakes.
Margarine	Add it to hot drinks in cold weather; make cookies; stir into hot cereals; add to grain dishes.
Powdered Eggs	Make Quiche, Chili Relleno Casserole, Phil's Power Dinner; add it to baking.
Powdered Milk	Add it to baked goods, cereals, casseroles, cream soups; try Phil's Power Dinner recipe or some hot milk drinks.

DIFFERENT CONSISTENCIES OF BATTER:

PANCAKE BATTER:

VERY THIN and RUNNY: WILL SPREAD QUICKLY TO FORM THIN PANCAKES.

MUFFIN BATTER:

THICKER and LUMPIER: WILL STILL POUR, BUT JUST BARELY!

BISCUIT DOUGH:

DOUGHY, TOO STICKY TO FALL OFF THE SPOON!
· FOR BREAD DOUGH: THICKEN FURTHER UNTIL DOUGH FORMS A BALL.

RECIPES

BEVERAGES • BREAKFASTS • DINNERS
BREADSTUFFS • DESSERTS AND SNACKS

BASIC COOKING TERMINOLOGY

Rehydrate	To restore water to a dried food. Generally hot water works best and fastest. In most cases, rehydration takes about 15 minutes.
Presoaking	Another name for rehydrating, used especially with beans, legumes, and barley. Presoaking cuts down on cooking time. Presoaking can take 2 hours to overnight.
Cream	Baking term to mix sugar and margarine together until totally integrated.
Cut In	Baking term to add margarine to a mixture of dry ingredients by using 2 knives or 2 spoons, slicing the margarine in opposite directions. End result is pea-sized bits of flour-covered margarine.
Bring to a Boil	To heat a liquid until it starts to bubble over the entire surface.
Simmer	To cook at low heat without boiling, only occasional bubbles on the surface.
Fry	To cook fairly quickly in hot grease in a pan, generally turning food halfway through cooking time. Food should be brown in color, but not burnt.
Sauté	Basically similar to frying, but using less oil and stirring the food as it cooks.
Dice	To cut up into small cubes.
Let rise	Baking term to allow a yeast product to double in size.
Twiggy fire	See chapter on cooking on fires.

Clock Method of Cooking

A rotation method of cooking, moving the pan "around the clock" to be sure all areas cook thoroughly.

TOP VIEW:

STEP 1

HOT!

HOT!

STEP 2

STEP 3

HOT!

GO AROUND AS MANY TIMES AS NEEDED TO BAKE THE CONTENTS.

MEASUREMENTS

All recipes in this cookbook are written with standard measurements.

1. "Tbs." stands for tablespoon.
2. "tsp." is teaspoon.
3. 3 level teaspoons equal 1 tablespoon.
4. 4 level tablespoons equal 1/4 standard cup.
5. 5 tablespoons + 1 teaspoon equal 1/3 standard cup.
6. 8 level tablespoons equal 1/2 standard cup.
7. 16 level tablespoons equals 1 standard cup.
8. "lb." stands for one pound dry weight.
9. "pkg." stands for package.
10. "pinch" is the amount of dry spice you can pick up between your thumb and first two fingers.
11. "dash" is the term used with spices to denote a quick shake of the bottle, allowing just a dusting of the spice out.
12. " (quotation marks) is the symbol for one inch.
13. A "heaping" teaspoon or tablespoon is filled as much as it can hold, "in a heap."

Because regular measuring cups and spoons are not used in the field, the following gives you some NOLS utensil equivalents:

1. A 12-ounce NOLS or other brand insulated mug filled to the top line equals 1 1/2 cups. (A 20-ounce mug equals 2 1/2 cups.)
2. NOLS Bakelite spoon equals 1 standard tablespoon.
3. Small NOLS spice bottle cap full equals 1 standard teaspoon.
4. Large NOLS spice bottle cap full equals 1 1/2 standard teaspoons.

If a recipe refers to "parts", it is an indication of proportions. For example, one part macaroni to two parts water means that whatever amount of macaroni you use, double the water—2 cups macaroni and 4 cups water.

BEVERAGES

Cowboy Coffee (serves 4)

6 cups cold water
4 - 6 Tbs. ground coffee

Bring water to a boil. Add coffee and set to side of fire where it will
stay hot but not boil. If using a cookstove, remove from heat and cover.
Coffee is done when grounds sink.

Cocoa Deluxe (1 serving)

1 1/2 cups hot water   *2 Tbs. cocoa mix*
1 - 2 Tbs. powdered milk   *1/2 tsp. vanilla*
dash of cinnamon

Mix cocoa mix and milk into hot water. Add vanilla and cinnamon. Stir.

Mocha Variation: make Cocoa Deluxe recipe above, substituting 1 1/2
cups coffee for hot water and adding brown sugar or honey to taste.

Hot Sweet Milk (1 serving)

1 1/2 cup hot water   *2 - 3 Tbs. powdered milk*
1/2 Tbs. honey or brown sugar   *1/2 tsp. vanilla*
dash of cinnamon

Mix powdered milk and sweetener into hot water. Add vanilla and
cinnamon and stir.

Super Tea (serves 4)

6 cups cold water   *3 Tbs. honey*
3 tea bags (Earl Grey, English Breakfast or other black tea)
3 Tbs. lemon drink mix or 4 Tbs. orange drink mix
4 whole cloves or pinch of ground cloves (optional)
pinch of cinnamon and nutmeg (optional)

Boil water in cooking pot. Add tea bags and steep until desired
strength. Stir in honey, fruit drink mix, and any spices.

Sun Tea (makes 1 quart)
To a NOLS one-quart (32-ounce) water bottle add 2 - 4 tea bags (more if herbal, less if regular tea).

Cover. Set in sun to steep. Time will vary depending on the day's temperature and location of tea jar.

Chai (1 serving)
1 1/2 cups hot water   1 - 2 Tbs. powdered milk
1 tea bag (Earl Grey, English Breakfast or other black tea)
brown sugar or honey to taste
cinnamon or mixed spices such as cloves and cardamom

Steep tea bag in boiling water. Add milk, sweetener and spices. Stir.

Variation: add 1/2 Tbs. butter or margarine.

Tea Variations (1 serving)
To 1 1/2 cups of boiling water add:
1. *peppermint tea bag to steep, and then stir in 2 Tbs. cocoa mix;*
2. *orange spice tea bag then add 1 Tbs. apple cider mix;*
3. *Earl Grey, English Breakfast or other black tea, add 1 Tbs. either orange or lemonade drink mix.*

Apple Cider (1 serving)
To 1 1/2 cups of hot water add 2 Tbs. apple cider mix.
Variation: to above recipe add 1/2 Tbs. either orange or lemonade drink mix and a dash of cinnamon or spice mix.

Hot Gelatin Drink (1 serving)
1 1/2 cups hot water
2 - 3 Tbs. gelatin mix such as lemon, lime, orange, etc.

Add gelatin to boiling water. Stir.

BREAKFASTS

Wouldn't Mom be happy to see you eating a good breakfast? When camping, you can choose from many different traditional breakfast foods, or you can reheat the previous night's leftovers or come up with some creative never-before-imagined recipes of your own.

CEREALS

Cereals can be eaten hot or cold. Besides hot cereals like oatmeal and Cream of Wheat, NOLS issues Shredded Wheat, Grapenuts, Cracklin' Oat Bran and assorted granolas. All of these are versatile; they can be eaten plain by the handful as a trail food, with cold milk for cold cereal, or with hot milk to make a fast hot cereal.

Cooked Cereals

Instant flake type cereals:
1 part cereal
2 parts water
1 tsp. salt/quart of water

Non-Instant granular type
cereals: (oatmeal, Cream
of Wheat, Rice, etc.)
1 part cereal
4 parts water
1 tsp. salt/quart of water

Boil water; add salt. Gradually pour in cereal while stirring. Stir while cooking until it reaches desired consistency. Or take off heat and steam with lid on. Instant cereals take 2-5 minutes to cook; non-instant take 10-15 minutes. To the cooked cereal, add margarine, milk, sugar, fruit and nuts in any combination.

Granola (makes 1 1/2 pounds)

Good as hot or cold cereal or as a trail food. Use quickly in hot weather.

5 Tbs. margarine
3 cups uncooked oatmeal
1/3 - 1/2 cup brown sugar or honey (depending on sweetness of fruit)
1/2 tsp. salt (if nuts used are unsalted)
1 cup dried fruit (good combination is chopped apricots, dates & pineapple)
1 cup nuts and seeds (chopped walnuts, almonds, & sunflower seeds, etc.)

Chop fruit and put into a bowl; add water to cover. Melt margarine in a frying pan. Add uncooked oatmeal, stirring to coat with margarine. Sprinkle brown sugar over the top; add drained fruit and nuts. Keep stirring until oatmeal is fried to a golden brown.

Variation: Use 1/2 cup honey as the sweetener to which you have added 2 Tbs. peanut butter. Try raisins and peanuts as your add-ins.

Muesli (makes 6 cups)

A cold cereal of oatmeal and fruit that can sit overnight for the morning's breakfast.

3 cups oatmeal
1/4 cup sunflower seeds
1/4 cup walnut or almonds, chopped
1 1/2 cups powdered milk
5 cups water
1/2 tsp. salt
1 cup dried fruit (chopped dates, apricots and raisins make a good mix)
2 tsp. cinnamon or a mix of spices such as cinnamon, nutmeg, etc.

Mix all ingredients together in a pot. Allow to sit 4 hours or overnight. This makes a very creamy cereal, naturally sweetened by the dried fruits.

You can also add wheat germ, bran, or brewer's yeast for an even more nutritious breakfast.

PANCAKES

Sierra Adare's Baking Mix (makes 4 1/4 cups)

The following recipe makes an all-purpose Bisquik-type product which can be used, with slight variations, in many different ways. Any recipe in this book which lists "baking mix" as one of its ingredients refers to this recipe. Make up a batch and keep it in a plastic bag ready to use.

4 cups flour
2 1/2 Tbs. baking powder
1/4 cup dry powdered milk
2 tsp. salt

Mix all ingredients together. Store in bag until needed.

Basic Pancakes

2 parts baking mix (see above)
1 part flour or uncooked cereal
enough water for a pourable batter

Stir baking mix and flour or dry cereal together. Add water gradually until you reach a pourable consistency. Lightly grease your frying pan and heat until a few drops of water dropped in the hot pan "skitter" on the surface. Pour or spoon batter into pan and cook gently over medium heat until the bubbles on the top surface set. Flip and cook other side. Serve with margarine, peanut butter-honey spread, brown sugar-margarine syrup or stewed fruit.

Variation: add chopped fruit or nuts, raisins, carob or chocolate chips to batter before cooking.

Brown Sugar-Margarine Syrup (makes 1/4 cup)

3 Tbs. margarine   *3 Tbs. brown sugar*
1 tsp. vanilla

Melt margarine. Add brown sugar and heat, stirring until sugar dissolves. Remove from heat and add vanilla. Serve at once over pancakes or hot cereal. If allowed to sit the brown sugar may harden and separate from the margarine. Reheat to reliquify.

Gingerbread Pancakes (makes 10-12 3" cakes)

1 cup baking mix* (see recipe index)   *3/4 to 1 cup water*
1 tsp. oil or melted margarine   *1/2 cup gingerbread mix*

Mix dry ingredients together. Add water gradually, stirring until mixture is thin enough to pour. Add the oil. Cook pancakes as in Basic Pancake recipe above.

*Note: If you use a commercial baking mix, omit the oil.

Donna's Hash Brown Fritters (makes 8 3" cakes)

1 cup hash browns, dry   *1 - 2 tsp. dried onion*
3 heaping Tbs. powdered milk   *3 Tbs. powdered egg*
2 Tbs. flour   *1 tsp. salt*
dash of pepper   *hot water*

Put hash browns and dried onions into a bowl. Cover with about one inch of water and rehydrate for 15 minutes. They should be a little firm. In another bowl, stir together dry ingredients. Drain water from potatoes and add 6 Tbs. of it gradually to flour mixture, mixing well. Add this mixture to the potatoes. Drop by large spoonfuls onto greased, heated frying pan. Flatten each cake. Cook about 3 minutes on each side. Serve with brown sugar syrup, stewed apples, cheese and hot sauce, or reconstituted sour cream mix.

Corn Pancakes (makes 10-12 3" cakes)

1 cup cornmeal
1/2 tsp. salt
2 Tbs. oil or melted margarine

1/2 cup powdered milk
1 Tbs. brown sugar
1 1/2 cups water

Combine cornmeal, milk and salt. Add water, oil, and brown sugar; mix well. Bake on hot, oiled frying pan. Good with brown sugar syrup or stewed fruit.

Cous-Cous Cakes (makes about 10-12 3" cakes)

1 cup cous-cous
1/3 cup powdered eggs
1 Tbs. baking powder
1 Tbs. margarine
enough hot water to make a cookie dough consistency

1/4 cup bulgar soy grits
1/3 cup powdered milk
1/2 Tbs. salt

Mix all ingredients except water in a pan. Slowly add hot water and stir well. Let sit for 10 minutes or more to absorb moisture and get fluffy. Melt margarine in fry pan. Form mixture into flat cakes. Fry on both sides until golden brown. Serve with brown sugar syrup, cheese and Spike, or a flavored white sauce.

Oatmeal Hotcakes (makes about 12 cakes)

2 cups oatmeal
1/4 tsp. cinnamon
1/4 cup raisins
1/4 cup dates, chopped small

1/2 cup powdered milk
1/4 tsp. salt
1 1/2 cups water

Using the butt of a spice bottle, grind the oatmeal to a flour-like consistency with some small pieces still left. Combine all ingredients with water and let soak overnight. To cook: form into 3 inch cakes about 3/4 inch thick and fry slowly in a little hot oil.

Whole Wheat Pancakes (makes about 12 3" cakes)

1 cup whole wheat flour
1 heaping Tbs. powdered eggs
1 heaping Tbs. powdered milk
1/2 tsp. baking powder
3 heaping Tbs. margarine, melted

1 cup white flour
pinch of salt
1 tsp. vanilla
1/2 tsp. cinnamon
3 cups warm water

Mix all dry ingredients together. Add melted margarine to hot water and slowly stir into dry ingredients. Stir well to prevent lumps. Heat frying pan and add 1/2 Tbs. margarine. Fry cakes on both sides until golden brown. Serve with brown sugar and margarine or stewed fruit. Good cold for trail food.

BREAKFAST GRAINS

Breakfast Cous-Cous (or Bulgar Variation)* (serves 4)

4 cups water   *2 cups cous-cous*
1/4 tsp. salt   *1/4 cup margarine*
3 Tbs. brown sugar or honey   *1/2 - 1 tsp. cinnamon*
1/4 cup walnuts, almonds, sunflower seeds or other nuts
2 Tbs. powdered milk mixed with 4 Tbs. water
1/4 cup raisins, dates, apricots or other fruit, chopped

Bring water to a boil with salt, brown sugar, margarine and fruit. Add cous-cous and milk mixture and stir. Cover and simmer for 5 to 10 minutes, stirring occasionally. When water is gone and mixture has fluffed up, mix in the cinnamon.

Variation: for Breakfast Bulgar substitute 2 cups water and 1 cup bulgar for cous-cous and water in above recipe; reduce sugar and margarine to 2 Tbs. each; use either 1/2 tsp. cinnamon or apple pie spice; optional: stir in 1 tsp. vanilla and 2 Tbs. peanut butter when done.

Hot Sweet Rice (serves 1)

1 cup leftover rice (warm or cold)   *1/4 - 1/2 cup hot milk*
1/2 Tbs. brown sugar or honey   *dash of cinnamon*
2 Tbs. raisins or other fruit or nuts   *1/2 Tbs. margarine*

To hot milk add the margarine, brown sugar and cinnamon. Mix fruit and nuts into the rice. Pour hot milk over top. Stir and eat.

OTHER BREAKFAST RECIPES

Bagels

Bagels are a versatile food for breakfast or snacking. They can be spread with margarine and toasted face down in a frying pan, or spread with cream cheese, or peanut butter and honey.

Variations:

1.   Cheese Bagels—fry bagel halves face down in 2 Tbs. margarine in a fry pan. Flip over and layer with cheese. Cover and cook over medium heat for 2-3 minutes. Sprinkle with Spike or hot sauce.

2.   Bacon Bagels—fry bacon and remove from pan. Fry bagel halves face down in bacon fat. Flip over and layer with cheese. Cover pan and cook for 2-3 minutes until cheese melts. Add crumbled bacon to top. Good with hot sauce or cayenne pepper.

Hash Browns With Cheese (serves 2)

1 1/2 cups hash browns, dry   *hot water*
1/2 cup cheese cubes or grated cheese   *1 Tbs. margarine*
salt and pepper to taste

Put hash browns into a sauce pan. Cover with one inch of hot water and rehydrate for 15 minutes. Drain off excess water. Melt margarine in a hot fry pan. Add hash browns. Cook, stirring occasionally until browned. Stir in cheese and remove from heat. Cover and allow to sit until cheese is melted. Good with hot sauce or picante. Salt and pepper to taste.

Variation: add ham or bacon bits; or rehydrate 1 Tbs. onion with hash browns and cook as above.

Omelet/Crepe (serves 1)

Filling:
2 Tbs. powdered egg   *3 Tbs. potato pearls*
1 Tbs. powdered milk   *1 Tbs. dried onions*
1 Tbs. baking mix   *1 tsp. soy sauce*
about 1/2 cup water   *1/3 cup cheese, cubed or grated*

In a bowl mix dry egg, milk and baking mix together. Add water gradually, stirring to keep from lumping. Pour a small amount of hot water over onions and let rehydrate. Melt 1 Tbs. margarine in hot frying pan. Pour in egg mixture and swirl around so it covers entire bottom of pan. Cover and cook over medium to low heat. It will set quickly. In bowl mix potato pearls, drained onions, and cheese with enough hot water to make a smooth mixture. Stir in the soy sauce. Spread this over half the omelet. Fold other side over potatoes and cook a minute to heat up. Try this with a few drops of hot sauce or picante.

Variation: try using stewed fruit for your filling, or add ham or bacon bits to the potato filling.

DINNERS

PASTAS

Basic Pasta Recipe (serves about 3)

2 parts water (4 cups)   *1 part pasta (2 cups)*
1 tsp. salt per quart of water or to taste

Add pasta to boiling water; boil gently 10-15 minutes. Drain water and save for soups. Add any of a variety of sauces to cooked pasta.

Hint: When cooking pasta, watch it carefully as it can go quickly from "still chewy" to "mushy." Drain it immediately when cooked as leaving it in the water, even if pan is removed from heat, will continue the cooking process. Adding 1 tsp. of oil or margarine to cooking water will prevent pasta from cementing together when the water is drained.

Basic Pasta Casserole (serves 3-4)

4 cups water   *2 cups pasta*
1 tsp. salt (if needed)   *1/2 cup powdered milk*
spices and bases (see chart)   *1/4 cup water*
3 Tbs. margarine
2 Tbs. dried vegetables (or 1/2 cup fresh, chopped in small pieces)
1 - 2 Tbs. thickener such as flour or potato pearls

Add vegetables to 4 cups water and bring to a boil. (If fresh vegetables, boil about 5 minutes.) Add pasta, bases, and spices. Gently boil for 8-15 minutes, stirring occasionally to prevent sticking. When pasta is done remove from heat. Do not drain as the small amount of liquid left is used in the sauce. Add any meat ingredients and margarine. Mix powdered milk and thickener in a bowl, add water (hot if using potato pearls) slowly , stirring to prevent lumps. Add to pasta and stir until it forms a sauce. Taste and add some salt if needed. Garnish with salad gems or sunflower seeds if desired.

Variation: Add 1/4 - 1/2 cup milk (liquid) or water to above recipe and bake 10-15 minutes in hot coals or on medium heat.

PASTA CASSEROLE :

IDEAS!

IDEAS!

CASEROLE	BASE	SPICES	OTHER INGREDIENTS
		PICK ONE OR MORE	CHOOSE ONE OR MORE
CHICKEN PASTA	CHICKEN	BLACK PEPPER, CURRY, THYME, OREGANO	CANNED CHICKEN, PEAS & CARROTS, PEANUTS, RAISINS
BEEF PASTA	BEEF	BLACK PEPPER, CHILI POWDER, CUMIN, GARLIC	ONION, BACON BITS, PEAS & CARROTS, MIXED VEGETABLES, PEPPERS
TOMATO PASTA	TOMATO	OREGANO, BASIL, GARLIC, BLACK PEPPER	ONIONS, GREEN and RED PEPPERS, MIXED VEGETABLES.
FISH OR TUNA	FISH STOCK OR VEGETABLE CUBE/ BOUILLON	BLACK PEPPER, DRY MUSTARD, DILL	BONED FISH OR TUNA, ONIONS, PEAS & CARROTS, MIXED VEGETABLES
BEEF STROGANOFF	BEEF	BLACK PEPPER, DRY SOUR CREAM MIX.	ONIONS, BACON BITS

Macs and Cheese (serves 3-4)

4 cups water
2 cups pasta
1 tsp. salt
black pepper and garlic to taste
2 Tbs. onions or other dried vegetables if desired

3 - 4 Tbs. margarine
4 Tbs. powdered milk
1 cup cheese chunks

Add salt and vegetables to water. Bring to a boil. Add pasta; boil 8-15 minutes, stirring occasionally. Drain out any water in excess of 1/4 cup. Add cheese and margarine; stir. Add enough water to powdered milk to make a thick liquid. Add it and any spices to pasta. Cook and stir until cheese is melted.

Bulgar-Miso Lasagne (serves 4)

1 recipe of Bulgar-Miso Sauce (see recipe index)
Cooked pasta for 4, drained
1 1/2 cups thinly sliced cheese

In oiled fry pan layer as follows: cheese, pasta, sauce. Repeat layer. Top with cheese. Cover and bake for about 15 minutes, using "clock" method until heated through.

Gado-gado Spaghetti (serves 2-3)

A spicy peanut butter sauce makes this a light, different spaghetti dish that is excellent hot, but especially good cold.

1/2 lb. spaghetti
3 Tbs. peanut butter
3 Tbs. soy sauce*
1 Tbs. dried onion, rehydrated
1/2 Tbs. chicken base or 1 packet
*   chicken broth or 1 vegetable cube*
3 Tbs. + 1 tsp. oil (corn oil is especially good)
sliced green or wild onions if available

1/4 tsp. garlic
3 Tbs. brown sugar
2 Tbs. sunflower seeds
3 Tbs. vinegar

*NOTE: due to bases, peanut butter and soy sauce, this dish can have a fairly salty taste. You can reduce the amount of soy sauce, but it is an important ingredient. It would be better to cut back or eliminate the base if you are concerned about saltiness.

Break pasta in half and put into boiling *unsalted* water to which 1 tsp. of oil has been added. Cook until done; drain immediately. In a fry pan, heat 3 Tbs. oil and add the sunflower seeds and rehydrated onions. Cook and stir over medium heat for 2 minutes. Add peanut butter and stir. DO NOT BURN!

In a bowl, mix the chicken base with the brown sugar, garlic and 3/4 cup water. Stir into peanut butter mixture. Add the vinegar and soy sauce. To eat this hot, heat the sauce thoroughly and pour over hot spaghetti.

This recipe is really designed to be best cold, and it loses some of its saltiness as it sits. Mix sauce and spaghetti and let cool. If available, sliced green or wild onions as a garnish really adds to the flavor.

RICE

When cooking rice or grains, put a spoon into the pot, gently push the grain aside and look at the bottom to check for doneness; do not overstir as it will become starchy.

Basic Recipe (serves 2)

2 cups water   *1/2 tsp. salt*
1/2 Tbs. margarine
1 cup rice, rinsed to remove some of the starch

Add salt to water and bring to a boil. Add rice and margarine and return to boiling. Cover and reduce heat. Simmer for 20-30 minutes.

Fried Rice

Cook rice as above. Rinse with cold water and drain well. Melt margarine in frying pan. Add any spices such as curry, garlic or cinnamon. Fry rice until golden brown, 10-15 minutes. Do not overload pan as it increases frying time. One tsp. chicken or beef base added to margarine gives you chicken or beefy fried rice.

Rice Casseroles

All casserole recipes under Pastas can be made substituting rice for the pasta.

Sweet and Sour Curried Rice (serves 3-4)

2 1/2 cups water
1 cup rice   *1 - 2 tsp. curry powder*
1 tsp. salt   *1/4 tsp black pepper*
1/2 cup raisins   *2 Tbs. dried onion*
2 Tbs. dried green and red peppers   *3 Tbs. soy sauce*
1/4 cup water   *3 - 5 Tbs. brown sugar or*
2 Tbs. margarine   *   3 - 4 Tbs. honey*
1/2 cup other dried fruit, chopped (try pineapple, apricots, dates, or
*   banana chips)*
1/2 cup nuts and seeds (try sunflower seeds, walnuts, peanuts
*   almonds)*
4 Tbs. vinegar (omitting removes "sour" element but results are still
*   good)*

Put water, rice, salt, raisins, dried fruit, dried onions and peppers into a pan. Cook, covered, until rice is done. Drain if necessary. Add nuts and spices and fry in margarine 5 to 10 minutes.

Mix vinegar, brown sugar, soy sauce and 1/4 cup water together. Stir thoroughly into rice. Simmer a few minutes with the cover on. Serve.

Variation: Use 1/2 cup rice and 1/2 cup bulgar.

Rice Nut Loaf

A hit with our tasters when served hot and when served cold.

1 1/2 cups cooked white or brown rice	*1/2 cup flour*
3/4 cup chopped walnuts	*1/2 tsp. salt*
1/4 cup chopped sunflower seeds	*4 Tbs. powdered eggs*
1 Tbs. dried onion, rehydrated	*6 Tbs. water, approximately*
* in hot water*	

1 cup shredded or small-diced cheese (cheddar and jack both are good)

Mix all ingredients together, adding water last in an amount that will moisten all the ingredients just enough to hold them together. Form a round loaf about 1 inch thick and place in the center of your oiled fry pan. (Or use an 8 or 9 inch loaf pan.) Cover and bake over medium heat for 30-50 minutes. Let sit 10 minutes before slicing. Good hot or cold, plain or with a flavored white sauce.

Spanish Rice with Beans (serves 3)

1/2 cup white rice, presoaked	1/2 tsp. salt
1/2 cup pinto beans, presoaked*	1 tsp. garlic powder
3 - 4 1/2 cups water	2 heaping Tbs. tomato base
2 Tbs. dried green and red pepper	2 Tbs. chili powder
1 Tbs. dried onions	1 cup cheese, cubed
1/4 - 1/2 tsp. cumin (optional)	

Start with 3 cups water and add more if necessary. Put all ingredients, except cheese, together in a pot. Cover and bring to a boil. Stirring often to prevent burning, cook 20-30 minutes until rice and beans are soft and most of the water is absorbed. Turn off heat, add cheese and cover for a few minutes to let cheese melt. Great with tortillas.

Variation: If using bean powder, add rice and all other ingredients except beans and cheese to 1 1/2 cups water. Cook as directed. Add 1 cup bean powder to 2 cups water and cook until thick. Stir into the rice mixture when you add the cheese.

Seasoned Rice in Fruit and Nut Curry Sauce (serves 2)

1 Tbs. margarine   *1 Tbs. dried onions*
2 - 3 Tbs. dried peas and carrots   *1/4 tsp. garlic*
1 cup rice   *2 cups water*
1 tsp. soy sauce   *1 tsp. vinegar (optional)*
2 tsp. curry
1/2 Tbs. chicken base or 1 chicken
broth packet or 1 vegetable bouillon cube

Sauce:
1 cup white sauce made without salt (see recipe index)
1 tsp. brown sugar   *2 tsp. soy sauce*
1/2 - 1 tsp. curry powder
2 Tbs. raisins or other chopped dried fruit
2 Tbs. chopped almonds or other nuts
dash of cumin (optional)
cayenne or hot sauce to taste

Mix all rice ingredients except soy and vinegar in a fry pan. Cover and cook 20-30 minutes until rice is done. Stir in soy sauce and vinegar. Make white sauce; add all other sauce ingredients except cayenne or hot sauce; blend and cook until heated through. Mix sauce into rice or pour over individual bowls. Add cayenne or hot sauce to taste.

Variation: Add one can of chicken to the rice as it cooks.

Hint: If the whole group likes curry, add it to both the rice and sauce to taste. If some don't like it, omit it from the rice and let them eat rice with soy instead of curry sauce.

GRAINS

Cous-cous

Cous-cous is a very nutritious durum wheat product common in the North African desert countries and Europe. It fits well into the NOLS food program because it is inexpensive, tastes great and cooks quickly. It resembles millet in color, grits in texture and rice in its cooked state. Good for breakfast or dinner.

Claudia's Favorite Cous-cous Pilaf (serves 4)

2 cups dry cous-cous
4 cups water
1 Tbs. chicken base or 1-2 broth packets or cubes
2-4 Tbs. dried vegetables (peas and carrots are good)
1-2 cups cubed cheddar or jack cheese
4 Tbs. margarine (or more to taste)

Bring water, chicken or other base and dried vegetables to a rolling boil. Add cous-cous and margarine. Stir well; cover and cook on low for 10-15 minutes. Check frequently as can burn easily. Once grain is dry and light, remove from heat. Stir in cheese; cover for a few minutes until cheese is melted. Serve with soy or hot sauce.

Bulgar

Bulgar is cracked wheat that has been par-boiled, then dried. The bulgar NOLS issues has soy grits (course ground soybeans) added to make a more nutritional food. The protein of the bulgar and soy compliment each other, making a "complete protein." Bulgar is also a versatile food. It cooks up quickly and can be eaten as a breakfast cereal or a dinner food like rice or cous-cous, or added to bread and pancakes in place of part of the flour. Below is the ratio of bulgar to water for cooking (same as for rice or cous-cous).

1 cup bulgar-soy grits
2 cups water

Bulgar-Rice Pilaf (serves 3-4)

1 cup bulgar or bulgar soy grits　　　*1 cup rice*
4 cups water (seasoned with any base)　*1 Tbs. dried onion*
2 Tbs. dried mixed vegetables　　　　*3 heaping Tbs. margarine*
1/2 cup cubed cheese

Add all ingredients except cheese to a pot. Cook, covered, over medium heat for 20 minutes. Stir as little as possible. When dry and fluffy, add cheese and scoop into oiled fry pan; fry until browned.

Spanish Bulgar (serves 3-4)

1 cup bulgar soy grits
1 Tbs. dried onion
1/2 cup tomato base
1/2 tsp. black pepper
1 Tbs. chili powder or more to taste

2 cups boiling water
4 Tbs. margarine
1 Tbs. oregano
1 cup cubed cheese
1 tsp. garlic powder

Add boiling water to bulgar and onion. Cover and let stand 15 minutes. Melt margarine in frying pan, add bulgar, spices and tomato powder. Mix well. Add sufficient water to keep from sticking. Put cheese on top, cover and lower heat. Serve when mixture is dry and fluffy and cheese is melted.

Tabouli Salad

2 cups bulgar soy grits
2 1/2 cups boiling water
2 Tbs. parsley flakes
1/2 cup oil
2 - 3 Tbs. dried mixed vegetables

1 tsp. salt
1/4 - 1/2 tsp. pepper
5 Tbs. lemon juice
1 Tbs. dried onion
1 peppermint tea bag

Place bulgar, 2 cups of boiling water, dried onion and dried vegetables in a pot. Steep tea bag in remaining 1/2 cup of water for 2-3 minutes. Discard tea bag and add water to bulgar. Let sit for 1/2 hour. Add remaining ingredients. Stir well. Allow to sit another 1/2 hour before eating.

Polenta

Polenta is a special Italian grind of corn. Cornmeal works well as a substitute. It cooks up thick and can be eaten sweet or spicy.

Basic Polenta Recipe (serves 3-4)

1 cup cornmeal   1 tsp. salt
2 Tbs. margarine (optional)
3 - 4 cups water (4 if you want it as a hot cereal, 3 if you want it firmer for fried cakes)

Mix salt and cornmeal in a pan. Add water gradually, stirring to prevent lumps. Bring to a boil, then reduce heat and simmer 5 to 10 minutes, stirring often. Be careful cooking this as it can spew out hot cornmeal lava bombs if heat is too high. Stir in margarine.

To serve: add raisins or other fruit, brown sugar or honey, and nuts. Or try parmesan or crumbled cheddar, sunflower seeds and hot sauce.

Fried Polenta Cakes

Let cooked polenta cool for a while to thicken, then form into cakes or cut into slices. Fry on both sides in margarine in a hot pan. Serve plain or with honey.

Variations:
1. Fry on one side, turn, spread top with a sauce made of 1 part tomato base to 2 parts water, and sprinkle with crumbled cheese; continue cooking until cheese melts.
2. Mix 2 Tbs. powdered egg with 3 Tbs. water. Pat onto cakes and then roll them in either a cornmeal and flour mix, or ground up oatmeal or wheat germ with salt and pepper. Fry until brown, turning once.
3. Serve cooked cakes with a garlic-cheese sauce.

Falafel

Falafel is a Middle Eastern staple made of ground chick peas (garbanzo beans), yellow peas, whole wheat flour, onion, baking powder and spices. Because it can be rather dry, it is best served with a sauce or, if car camping, in pita bread with lettuce, tomato, cucumber and plain yogurt or Tahini Sauce.

Basic Falafel Recipe (serves 2-3)

1 cup falafel mix
oil for frying
3/4 cup water

Stir water thoroughly into mix and allow to sit 10 minutes. Shape into small patties and fry on both sides in hot oil to desired crispness. Serve with rice or pasta and a seasoned white sauce or gravy. Also good with cheese melted on top.

Variation: For a milder version mix half falafel with half cornmeal or flour.

Mixed Grain Balls (makes 22-25 balls)

Grain Balls can be eaten cold as a trail food or added to stews, served with egg noodles and gravy, or with spaghetti.

3/4 cup cornmeal	*1/2 tsp. garlic*
1/2 cup whole wheat flour	*1/2 tsp. salt*
1/4 cup white flour	*1 tsp. soy sauce*
6 Tbs. dry milk powder	*1 Tbs. oil*
1 Tbs dried onion	*1/2 - 3/4 cup water*

Mix all dry ingredients together. Rehydrate onions and add with remaining ingredients, mixing well to a stiff dough. Form 22-25 grain balls, approximately the size of a walnut. Add about 1 Tbs oil to a fry pan and heat. Add grain balls and shake around until they are coated with oil. Cover and cook 20-30 minutes, shaking occasionally to be sure they brown on all sides. Eat warm or cold. Good served over egg noodles with a white sauce seasoned with beef base and black pepper, or over spinach noodles with a chicken base flavored white sauce, or over spaghetti with a tomato-garlic sauce.

Your Choice Barley Dinner (serves 3-4)

4 cups water *2 Tbs. margarine*
1 vegetable bouillon packet or cube, or 1/2 - 1 Tbs. other base
1/4 - 1/2 cup crumbled cheese *1 Tbs. dried onions (optional)*
1 cup barley, presoaked if possible, or use "quick barley flakes"

Put water, vegetable cube, barley and onions into a pot. Bring to boil; reduce heat and cover. Simmer for 40-60 minutes (less for quick barley) over medium heat. Barley, when done, should be "springy" but not crunchy. Stir in cheese and margarine. Let sit for a few minutes and stir again. To serve, let everyone add his choice of spices such as: pepper, garlic, curry, spike, picante, garlic, oregano, soy sauce, chili powder.

Mexican Grits and Cheese Casserole (serves 4-6)

5 cups water *1 1/2 cups grits*
4-6 Tbs. margarine or bacon grease *2 tsp. chili powder*
1/2 cup water *Tabasco to taste*
2 tsp. salt *1 tsp. cumin (optional)*
1 - 1 1/2 tsp. garlic *salad gems (optional)*
1 1/2 cups cheese, grated or diced small
5 Tbs. powdered egg

Bring 5 cups water to a boil. Stir in grits and salt. Cook, stirring, until thickened. Mix egg with 1/2 cup water. Add to grits with spices, margarine and most of cheese. Pour into a greased fry pan. Cover with remaining cheese. Bake, covered over low heat 30-45 minutes. Serve garnished with salad gems for crunch and more Tabasco.

POTATOES
Basic Potato Recipe for One

1/3 cup potato pearls
margarine (optional)
2/3 - 1 cup boiling water

Put pearls in a bowl. Add boiling water gradually until it reaches desired consistency. Stir in margarine.

Variations:

1. Stir in grated or chunked cheese.
2. Good with bulgar-miso sauce (see recipe under sauces) over the top.
3. Make potatoes with less water, form into patties and fry in margarine. After turning, add slice of cheese to top and allow to melt. Good with hot sauce or picante.

Potato-Cheese Patties (makes 12 3" cakes)

2 cups water
1/2 - 1 cup crumbled or chunked cheese
1/2 cup powdered milk, dry
margarine for frying
1/2 cup baking mix (see recipe index)

1 cup potato pearls
2 Tbs. dried onions
pepper to taste
1/4 cup flour or cornmeal

Boil water with onions. Add to potato pearls and stir well. Allow to cool for about 5 minutes. Mix in all other ingredients except margarine and flour or cornmeal; form a stiff dough. Form dough into patties and roll them in the flour or cornmeal. Fry in margarine until both sides are slightly crisped. Good with picante or hot sauce or, if you're adventurous, with peanut butter!

Hint: shape patties while wearing 2 plastic bags (on your hands!)

BEANS AND LEGUMES

The following three recipes use regular or partially cooked beans. If you are using bean powder, you will have to adjust your cooking method. See "Variation" under each recipe. A general rule of thumb is 1 part bean powder to 2 parts water. Cook until soft and thick.

Hint: if necessary to add more water to cooking beans, use hot water. Adding cold will cause beans to blanch and will greatly extend the cooking time.

Spicy Beans and Macs (serves 4)

2 cups quick cooking pinto beans, presoaked*
5+ cups water
1 Tbs. dried onion
2 - 4 Tbs. dried green and red peppers
2 - 3 cup pasta (other than spaghetti)
salt, black pepper, garlic, oregano, chili powder to taste
1 Tbs. beef base or miso, or 1 vegetable bouillon cube or base packet

1 Tbs. margarine
cheddar or jack cheese

Add all ingredients except pasta and cheese to water. Cook until beans are tender. Mixture should be brothy so add more hot water if needed. Cooking time depends on elevation and whether beans were presoaked. When beans are nearly done, cook pasta separately. Drain it and stir into the beans. Add grated or chunked cheese to individual portions.

Variation: If using bean powder, cook 1 1/2 cups beans in 3 cups water. Follow recipe except cook pasta separately *as* beans are cooking.

Refried Beans and Tortillas (serves 2-3)

1 1/2 cups quick cooking pinto beans, presoaked*
4 cups water   *2 heaping Tbs. margarine*
3 Tbs. tomato base   *cheese cubes*
3 Tbs. powdered milk   *1 Tbs. dried onion*
tortillas (commercial or see recipe index)
chili powder, salt, pepper, and cumin to taste

Put beans, margarine, onions and water into a large pan. Cover and bring to a boil. Reduce heat and cook until beans are done, about 30 minutes. While beans are cooking put the tomato and milk powders into a cup, add some of the bean water slowly, stirring to prevent lumps. Stir it into the beans. Add seasonings. When beans are done, you can add cheese, cover and set aside, or add cheese later as you make up the individual servings. Fry tortillas on both sides in small amount of oil or margarine; the longer you fry them the crisper they get. Spoon beans onto tortillas. Add sunflower seeds or cooked red and green peppers if desired; sprinkle with hot sauce or picante (see recipe index).

Variation: If using bean powder, cook 1 1/2 cups beans in 3 cups water to which rehydrated onions and tomato powder have been added. Omit milk powder and margarine. Cook until thick. Refried bean powder already has spices added, but you can add more if you choose.

Clancy's Favorite (serves 4)

1 cup rice   *3 Tbs. margarine*
1/2 cup quick cooking beans*   *3 cups water*
1 Tbs. beef base or 1 - 2 base packets
1 cup chopped fruit (apricots, pineapple and raisins are good)
1 - 1 1/2 cups meat, such as cubed ham, cut up sausage, sauteed
  ground beef

Mix all ingredients together in a fry pan. Cover and cook over medium heat for about 20 minutes. Do not stir while cooking or it will become gummy. When water has been absorbed, test rice and beans for doneness. If too chewy, add a little more water and cook a few minutes more.

Variation: If using bean powder, add 1/2 cup beans to 1 cup boiling water. Cook about 5 minutes or until beans are no longer hard. Set aside. Mix rest of ingredients, reducing water to 2 cups. Cook as above. When done, stir beans into dinner and let heat for another minute.

Hint: to spice it up try 1/4 tsp. cumin or 1/4 - 1/2 tsp. dry mustard or 1/4 tsp. apple spice.

Black-eyed Peas and Bacon Stew (serves 3-4)

1 - 1 1/2 cups bacon, cut in one inch pieces
1 cup quick cooking black-eyed peas (or lima beans), presoaked
1/2 cup bulgar   *4 cups water*
1/4 - 1/2 tsp. black pepper   *4 Tbs. potato pearls*
1 Tbs. dried onions   *1/2 cup cubed or grated cheese*
1 Tbs. beef base or 1 vegetable bouillon cube

Fry bacon pieces until cooked but not crisp. Leave bacon and grease in pan; add peas, bulgar, water, onion and base. Bring to a boil; cover and reduce heat. Cook until beans are done, about 30 minutes. When beans are soft, stir in pepper. Stir potato pearls directly into stew if there is liquid left. If not, add boiling water to pearls in a bowl to make a very liquid consistency, then stir into stew. Sprinkle cheese over top, cover and let sit until cheese is melted. Good with hot sauce.

Variations:
1. Add 1/4 - 1/2 tsp. dry mustard and 1 Tbs. brown sugar or honey when you add the black pepper.
2. Substitute cubed ham for bacon, omit cooking it, just add to pan with beans, water, etc.

Black-eyed Peas and Barley Stew (serves 3)

1 cup barley   *1 Tbs. tomato base*
2 Tbs. dried green and red peppers
1 cup black-eyed peas   *1 Tbs. dried onion*
5 cups water   *2 Tbs. margarine*
1/2 Tbs. beef base, or miso, or 1 vegetable cube
salt, pepper and garlic to taste

Add all ingredients to water. Bring to boil. Cover, reduce heat and simmer about 30-40 minutes. Stir occasionally and add more water if necessary. It is done when beans are soft and barley still somewhat chewy.

Lentil Chili (serves 2-3)

1 cup lentils, presoaked
3 Tbs. tomato base
2 Tbs cornmeal (optional)
1 Tbs. chili powder
1 Tbs. dried onion

1 tsp. oregano
1 tsp. garlic powder
4 cups water
1 - 1/2 cup cheese cubes

Combine all ingredients except cheese. Bring to a boil; cover and reduce heat to medium. Simmer for about 30 minutes until lentils are soft. Fill individual bowls and top with cheese.

Lentil Casserole (serves about 3)

1 cup lentils, presoaked
1/2 - 1 tsp. salt (optional)
soy sauce to taste

1/2 - 1 cup cheese
1 cup potato pearls

Pour presoaked lentils into a pan. Add water to cover to about one inch. Stir in salt. Bring to boiling; cover and reduce heat. Cook at a slow boil for 15 to 30 minutes, until lentils are soft. Drain off juice and keep it. Use some of the juice to mix up the instant potatoes, adding soy sauce to taste. In your frying pan spread the potatoes in a layer, cover with the lentils. Top with crumbled or sliced cheese. Pour some of the lentil juice over the top to moisten the casserole. You can sprinkle top with sesame seeds, sunflower seeds or salad gems if desired. Cover and bake until cheese is melted and casserole is heated through. Good with NOLS Picante.

Lentil-Bulgar Casserole (served 3-4)

Follow the same directions for the Lentil Casserole above, only replace potatoes with cooked bulgar. This gives a different, more chewy texture to the casserole. You can add soy sauce or any spices you choose to the bulgar.

Lentil Rice Cakes (makes 8 3" cakes)

2/3 cup white rice
1/3 cup lentils, presoaked
2 cups water
1/4 tsp. oregano
soy sauce to taste

1 - 2 Tbs. white flour
1 tsp. salt
1 Tbs. dried onions
dash of garlic
margarine for frying

Put rice, lentils, water, salt and onions into a pot. Cook, covered, until lentils are soft, about 20-30 minutes. Stir in spices and soy sauce. Mash with spoon. Stir in flour to help hold it together. Form into patties. Fry in margarine until both sides are slightly crisped. Great with picante, Peanut-Miso sauce, or a flavored white sauce.

Variation: These are great made with brown rice but you will have a much longer cooking time unless you use a pressure cooker.

Gina's Confetti Salad (or Pasta Salad Variation)

This recipe can take several days to prepare due to need to sprout lentils.

1 cup lentils, sprouted   *1 Tbs. dried onion*
1 Tbs. tomato base   *water*
1 cup rice (or bulgar or white macaroni)
1 - 2 Tbs. dried green and red peppers

Dressing:
2 Tbs. oil   *3 - 4 Tbs vinegar*
1/4 - 1/2 tsp. garlic   *1/2 tsp. salt*
1/2 tsp. oregano and/or basil   *1/4 tsp. black pepper*
cayenne or hot sauce to taste

Soak lentils overnight then drain and leave in a warm spot to sprout. Put rice (or bulgar, or pasta), peppers, onions, tomato base and water in a saucepan. Cover and cook until rice is done. Allow to cool. Mix rice and sprouted lentils together. In a bowl or bottle, mix all dressing ingredients. Pour onto salad and mix in. Allow to sit for 30 minutes or longer for flavors to meld.

Variation: Add 1/2 to 1 cup cheese cubes, or if car camping, add fresh tomatoes, black olives, and replace dried onions and peppers with fresh ones.

FISH

Fish may be cleaned and cooked whole if small. If large or thick, they can be cut into 1/2 to 1 inch steaks or fillets. To fillet, hold fish by the tail and slice toward the head, cutting the meat off where it joins the bone. When one side is done, do the other.

   Hint: It's best not to put freshly caught fish in a plastic bag because they can get too warm. Their fats turn to oils and the flesh takes on a "fishy" aroma and taste.

Fried Fish (serves 1)

1 cleaned fish, slightly wet, either whole or cut into steaks or fillets
1/4 to 1/2 cup cornmeal   *1/2 tsp. salt*
spices such as black pepper, garlic powder, dill, dry mustard or
    curry to taste
oil or margarine for frying (oil gives better taste and crispiness)

Mix cornmeal, salt, and any desired spices in a plastic bag. Put in slightly wet fish and shake to coat. Remove fish and place it in hot oil or melted margarine in a frying pan. Fry slowly until tender and flakes apart. Several cuts on the back of a whole fish or turning it can prevent it from curling as it cooks.

Variation: Mix 1 Tbs. powdered egg with 2 - 3 Tbs. water and dip fish in this before coating with cornmeal.

Baked Fish (serves 1)

Throw a whole, cleaned fish directly on hot coals. Turn when done on first side and continue cooking. Take off coals and season with salt and pepper to taste.

Variation: Steaks or fillets can be sprinkled with seasoning on both sides and added to melted margarine in a covered fry pan. Bake for about 20-25 minutes or until flakes apart.

Boned Fish

If you just need the meat, boil the cleaned fish, head and all, for 10-15 minutes until the meat starts to fall off the bones. Remove fish from water and strip off meat with a knife or fingers. Discard bones but save water for stock.

Creamed Fish

Pour a white sauce made with vegetables and spices over fish that has been boiled, poached, or baked. A tomato sauce with onions, spiced cheese sauce or a white sauce with dill or mustard are good combinations.

Fish Patties (serves about 3)

Fish, boiled or poached and then boned
fish stock
1/3 - 1/2 cup dry powdered milk
1 - 2 Tbs. dried onions, boiled with fish

salt and pepper
1 1/2 cups potato pearls
margarine for frying

Cook fish in water with onions. Remove fish from stock, bone and flake the meat. To potato pearls, dry milk, salt and pepper, add enough of the fish stock to make a mashed potato consistency. Add flaked fish to this and mix well. Form into thick patties and fry on both sides in melted margarine. Serve with a white, cheese or dill sauce.

FILLET A FISH

METHOD 1

SIDE 1:

AVOID PUNCTURING INTERNAL ORGANS

MAKE A CUT DOWN TO THE BONE : DO NOT CUT HEAD OFF.

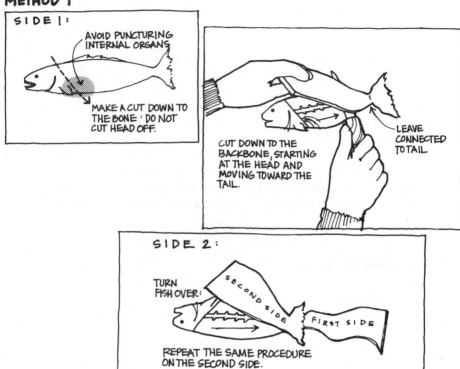

CUT DOWN TO THE BACKBONE, STARTING AT THE HEAD AND MOVING TOWARD THE TAIL.

LEAVE CONNECTED TO TAIL

SIDE 2:

TURN FISH OVER:

SECOND SIDE

FIRST SIDE

REPEAT THE SAME PROCEDURE ON THE SECOND SIDE.

METHOD 2

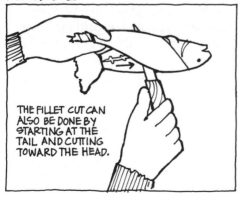

THE FILLET CUT CAN ALSO BE DONE BY STARTING AT THE TAIL AND CUTTING TOWARD THE HEAD.

Fish-Potato Casserole (serves 3-4)

2 cups dried potato slices or hash browns
1 - 2 cups boned fish   *2 Tbs. dried onions*
3 Tbs. margarine
2 - 3 cups white sauce (see recipe index) seasoned
   with salt and pepper to taste (the moister the casserole the better)

Put potatoes and onions in a large pot; cover with 1 inch of hot water
and rehydrate for 15 minutes. Drain water and use it to make the white
sauce. Melt 1 Tbs. margarine in frying pan. Add layer of drained
potatoes, layer of flaked fish, layer of white sauce. Repeat. Dot top with
remaining margarine. Sprinkle with salad gems or sunflower seeds if
desired. Cover pan and cook on medium heat for 20-25 minutes, using
"clock" method of rotating pan until potatoes are cooked and casserole
is bubbly.

Fish Chowders (serves 3-4)

Fish, cleaned   *8 cups water*
4 Tbs. dried onions   *1/2 cup margarine*
4 Tbs. other dried vegetables   *salt and pepper to taste*

For New England style add:
3/4 cup potato pearls   *2/3 cup dry powdered milk*

For Manhattan style add:
3-4 Tbs. tomato base   *1/4 - 1/2 tsp. oregano*
1/2 cup dry powdered milk (optional)

Cook fish in water with onions and vegetables until fish is ready to bone
(about 10-15 minutes). Remove fish, bone it and return fish to stock.
Spice to taste. Add margarine. Reduce heat to simmer. Add potatoes
and milk for New England style or tomato base, milk and oregano for
Manhattan style. Heat through and serve.

SPECIALITIES OF THE HOUSE

Mike Bailey's Piggies in a Snowdrift (serves 3-4)

2 cups ham, cubed   *1 cup cheese, sliced*
approximately 3/4 cup water   *2 Tbs. margarine*
1 1/2 cups Bisquik or baking mix (see recipe index)

Melt 1 Tbs. margarine in hot frying pan. Add ham and fry for 1-2 minutes. Place cheese slices over ham, cover pan and let cheese melt. Meanwhile mix Bisquik and water (or baking mix, 1 Tbs. margarine and water); adding water gradually to form a biscuitlike dough (holds form but is not stiff and dry). Spread dough over cheese and ham. Cover pan, reduce heat and bake for about 15 minutes until dough is cooked.

Phil's Power Dinner (serves 4)

2 cups bulgar or cous-cous   *2 Tbs. margarine*
1 - 2 Tbs. dried peas and carrots   *4 Tbs. flour*
4 - 6 Tbs. powdered eggs   *1 tsp. baking powder*
3/4 cup powdered milk   *1 tsp. salt*
1/4 tsp garlic powder   *1/4 tsp. black pepper*
water (4 cups + water for sauce)
1/2 - 1 cup grated or cubed cheese (optional)

Cook bulgar or cous-cous in four cups water to which 1/2 tsp. salt and dried vegetables have been added. When done, stir in margarine and cheese. Pour into your fry pan.

In a bowl, mix eggs, milk, flour, baking powder, 1/2 tsp. salt, pepper and garlic. Mix well. Gradually add water to make a sauce consistency (not a paste). Pour this over grain in fry pan, cover tightly and cook over medium heat, using clock method of rotation. Dish is done when topping is set and cooked through, about 20-30 minutes. Serve with soy sauce, Tabasco or picante.

Pizza (serves 1-2)

Yeast Crust (preferred)
1 tsp. dry yeast   *1/2 tsp. sugar*
1/4 tsp. salt   *1/2 cup lukewarm water*
1 cup flour (try 1/2 white, 1/2 whole wheat)

OR:

Quick Crust (more "doughy")

1/2 cup baking mix (see recipe index)	*1 Tbs. margarine*
1/2 cup flour	*1/2 cup cold water*

Sauce: Make one batch of Spaghetti Sauce, White Sauce with tomato base or Mexican Sauce (see recipe index).

Possible Toppings:
Fish, wild onions, bacon or ham bits, meat such as ham or sauteed ground beef, wild mushrooms*, jack, cheddar or mozzarella cheese, crumbled or thinly sliced. *Be sure you properly identify wild mushrooms before using.

For yeast crust—dissolve yeast in warm water with sugar and salt. Add flour and mix to a stiff dough. For quick crust—mix margarine into flour and baking mix with fingers. Mix in water to form a dough.

Oil a fry pan, spread dough with oiled fingers to form a crust. Turn up edges to hold sauce. Pour sauce over crust, top with cheese and any other toppings. Cover and bake on a stove on low heat until crust is golden brown, about 20-25 minutes. Or you can use a twiggy fire, which helps cook crust from top and bottom. Be sure to move pan in clock rotation quarter turns to bake all parts of pizza. Alternative cooking method: put crust in pan and cook for about 10 minutes; flip, spread with sauce and cheese, cover and continue cooking for another 10 minutes.

Cheese Bombs

1/2 cup flour	*1/4 cup baking mix*
1/4 cup powdered egg	*cheddar or jack cheese*

1/2 - 1 Tbs. chicken or beef base (or 1 base packet)
*seasoning of choice**

*Possible seasoning combinations include:
1. 2 tsp. Worchestershire sauce, 1/4 tsp. dry mustard (optional), and garlic;
2. Garlic, hot sauce or cayenne, and chili powder;
3. Chili powder, cumin, and hot sauce.

Mix all ingredients except cheese and water. Add water until mixture is thicker than pancake batter, but thinner than biscuit dough. Cut cheese in 1 inch squares about 1/2 inch thick. Dip in batter. Fry quickly on both sides in hot oil. Serve plain or with picante (see recipe index).

Quiche Morraine (serves 4-6)

Crust:
1 1/4 cups flour
1/3 cup margarine

1/2 tsp. salt
3 Tbs. water

Filling:
1 1/2 cups crumbled or diced cheese
2 Tbs. dried onion, rehydrated
1/8 - 1/4 tsp. Tabasco or cayenne
2 Tbs. dried green and red peppers,
   rehydrated

1 1/2 cups powdered milk
1 cup powdered egg
3 cups water
salt and pepper to taste

For crust: Mix flour and salt together. Cut in margarine, using 2 knives or spoon edges. Mix in water to form a dough. Roll out and fit into a fry pan.

For filling: Layer cheese on the bottom of the pie crust. Mix dry milk and egg powders in a bowl; slowly add water, stirring constantly to prevent lumping. Stir in vegetables and any seasonings. Pour into crust, cover and bake, using a twiggy fire on top, 30 minutes or until crust pulls away from side of pan and filling is set.

SOUPS

Soups are a good source of protein, fats and carbohydrates and can be a great way to use up leftover ingredients. They make a quick warm-up meal with a hearty bread accompaniment.

Basic Broth Soup (serves 4-6)

6 - 8 cups water
1 - 1 1/2 cups solid ingredients

spices to taste
3 - 4 Tbs. margarine

1 - 3 Tbs. base of choice or use boullion cubes or packets (see chart)
salt (be careful! Taste first and add sparingly)

Boil water; add bases to taste. Add solid ingredients. Vegetables and rice take 20-30 minutes to cook so add these first. Noodles take 10-15 minutes. Add spices while solids are cooking. When solids are done, stir in margarine and salt (if necessary).

NOTE: if using tomato base, add it after solid ingredients are cooked.

Basic Cream Soup variation: Thicken above recipe with potato pearls or 2 - 3 Tbs. flour mixed into 4 Tbs. water and added to the soup; mix 1/2 to 1 cup powdered milk into 1/2 cup water and stir into soup; heat through and serve.

78

BROTH or CREAM SOUPS : IDEAS!

SOUP	BASE	SPICES PICK ONE OR MORE	SOLID INGREDIENTS CHOOSE ONE OR MORE	CREAM SOUP THICKENERS OR SPECIAL ADDITIONS
BEEF VEGETABLE OR TOMATO BEEF VEGETABLE	BEEF OR ½ BEEF ½ TOMATO	BLACK PEPPER, CHILI POWDER, GARLIC, CUMIN OREGANO/ BASIL	MEAT, HAM, OR BACON BITS; PEAS & CARROTS, NOODLES, GRAIN, LEFTOVER COOKED BARLEY, ONIONS	NONE
CHICKEN VEGETABLE OR CHICKEN RICE	CHICKEN	BLACK PEPPER, CURRY MUSTARD POWDER	CHICKEN, VEGETABLES, ONION, RICE, NOODLES.	NONE
ONION	BEEF	PEPPER	ONIONS, PARMESAN OR JACK CHEESE	NONE
LENTIL	BEEF OR ½ BEEF ½ TOMATO	BLACK PEPPER, CURRY POWDER, VINEGAR, CUMIN, BROWN SUGAR, CHILI POWDER	BARLEY, BACON OR HAM BITS, ONIONS, PEPPERS, CARROTS.	NONE
TOMATO OR TOMATO RICE	TOMATO	BLACK PEPPER, OREGANO/ BASIL, GARLIC	RICE	FLOUR (OPTIONAL), MILK
CORN CHOWDER	VEGIE CUBE, CHICKEN	BLACK PEPPER, MUSTARD POWDER	PEAS, CORN, ONIONS	POTATO PEARLS OR FLOUR, MILK
CREAM OF CHICKEN	CHICKEN	BLACK PEPPER, MUSTARD POWDER	CHICKEN PIECES, RICE OR NOODLES	FLOUR (OPTIONAL), MILK
MINESTRONE	TOMATO	BLACK PEPPER, OREGANO/ BASIL, GARLIC	MACARONI, LENTILS, GRAINS, ONIONS, VEGETABLES	NONE

Potato Cheese Soup (serves 2-3)

1/2 cup potato pearls
1/2 cup powdered milk
2 Tbs. flour
2 Tbs. dried onion
4 cups water

1/2 tsp. salt
1/2 tsp. pepper
1 tsp. oil
1 cup crumbled cheddar

Put everything but potatoes and cheese into a pot. Bring to a boil, stirring often. Put potato pearls into a bowl and add enough of the hot soup to form a thin paste. Pour this back into the soup; stir. Add cheese and cook, stirring until melted. Serve hot with bread. Good with a dash of cayenne, hot sauce or dry mustard powder.

Cream of Peanut Soup (serves 4)

1 Tbs. dried onions, rehydrated
6 cups plus 1 cup water
1/4 tsp. black pepper
1/2 cup potato pearls
2 vegetable bouillon cubes, or 2 packets chicken broth, or
    1/2 Tbs. chicken base
chopped peanuts or sunflower seeds for garnish

3 Tbs. margarine
1 cup peanut butter
1 cup powdered milk

Put vegetable cubes, pepper and 6 cups water in a pot. In fry pan melt margarine, add rehydrated onions and saute them for 2 minutes. Add peanut butter and heat while stirring. Add 3 cups of vegetable stock water to peanut mixture, ONE cup at a time, stirring. Pour this back into the remaining stock and place pot over medium heat.

Stir remaining 1 cup of water into the powdered milk. Add this to the soup. When it is heated, slowly add potato pearls to soup, stirring constantly to prevent lumping. (Or you can put pearls into a bowl and add enough of soup to form a thin paste, then add it back into the soup). Heat soup through and serve garnished with peanuts or sunflower seeds.

Mini-Miso Soup (serves 1)

Good for digestion problems. Pour boiling water into a mug. Stir in miso to taste.

Miso Soup with Vegetables (serves 3)

1 Tbs. dried onion or 1 medium onion, diced
2 Tbs. dried peas and carrots or 2 carrots, diced
4 1/2 cups water   *2 Tbs. margarine*
1 - 2 Tbs. miso

Rehydrate onions, peas and carrots for about 5 minutes. Melt margarine in pot. Add vegetables and saute about 2-3 minutes. Add water and heat to boiling. If using fresh vegetables, boil until tender. Put miso into a bowl; add some of the soup and blend. Pour miso back into soup and stir. Serve.

You're Not Going To Believe It Soup (serves 2-3)

1 cup oatmeal   *1 tsp. garlic powder*
5 Tbs. margarine   *4 cups water*
1 Tbs. dried onion   *1 vegetable bouillon cube*
2 Tbs. tomato base   *cumin and cayenne-optional*

Brown oats for about 5 minutes in a dry skillet over medium heat. DO NOT BURN! Set oats aside. Melt margarine and saute rehydrated onion. Add remaining ingredients except oatmeal and bring to a boil. Add oatmeal and boil for about 6 minutes. Serve plain or with a dash of cumin and cayenne.

SAUCES

Your imagination in sauce making can often spell the difference between a so-so meal and a great one. A basic white sauce takes on many different personalities with the addition of spices, bases, dried vegetables and cheese.

Basic White Sauce (makes about 1 cup)

3 Tbs. margarine or bacon grease   1 cup water or milk
3 Tbs. flour (white makes a lighter sauce)
Salt and pepper to taste (omit salt if you plan to add a base)

Melt margarine in a sauce pan. Stir in flour and let it cook for a few minutes, being careful not to burn it. Add water or milk, slowly, stirring to mix. Season with salt and pepper and cook until thickened and heated through.

Sauce Variations:
To the completed white sauce add one of the following:

1. 2 Tbs. tomato base, garlic, 1/4 tsp. oregano and/or basil for an Italian sauce;
2. 1/2 Tbs. chicken or beef base for a gravy good with mixed vegetables and noodles;
3. 2 Tbs. cheese base, 1/4 tsp. dry mustard powder, dash black pepper;
4. 1 - 2 tsp. curry powder for an Indian style sauce with rice and raisins;

5. 1 cup grated or cubed cheese;
6. 1 - 2 packets of Cup-of-Soup mixes.

NOTE: taste your sauce after adding a base. It may be salty enough without adding salt. The longer the sauce cooks, the thicker it gets so you may need to add more liquid, especially in these variety sauces. It can help smooth out the consistency and dilute excess salt flavor.

No-Cook Picante Sauce (makes about 1 cup)

The test panel gave this a rave review!

1 Tbs. dried onions
dash of garlic powder
1 Tbs. dried green and red peppers
1 cup water (1/2 hot and 1/2 cold)
1/4 tsp. hot sauce or cayenne (or to taste)
1 tsp. each vinegar and brown sugar (optional but adds good flavor)

2 Tbs. tomato base
dash of black pepper

Rehydrate onions and peppers in 1/2 cup hot water. Add tomato base and stir until well mixed. Add remaining ingredients and 1/2 cup cold water. Mix well. You can thin this out further if you wish. Serve cold over nachos, main dishes, potato-cheese patties, bean and lentil dishes, etc.

Spicy Peanut Gado-gado Sauce

Great change of pace for noodles or rice. See Gado-gado spaghetti recipe under pastas for sauce procedure.

Peanut-Miso variation: stir 1 Tbs. miso into sauce for peanut-miso flavor.

Bulgar-Miso Sauce

1 cup bulgar
1/4 - 1/2 tsp. oregano
1/4 - 1/2 tsp. garlic
1/2 - 1 tsp. basil

4 cups water
1/2 Tbs. miso
2 - 3 Tbs. tomato base

Cook bulgar in water until it's soft. Dissolve miso in some water in a bowl, set aside. Add remaining ingredients to bulgar and cook for a few minutes to heat through. Add miso. Good with pasta, mashed potatoes, rice-nut loaf, etc.

Spaghetti Sauce (makes about 1 1/2 cups)

1 Tbs. dried onion
1 Tbs. dried green and red pepper
1/2 tsp. oregano and/or basil
1 1/2 cup water, approximately
2 Tbs. powdered milk (optional)

1/4 tsp. black pepper
1/4 - 1/2 tsp. garlic
4 - 6 Tbs. tomato base

Rehydrate onions and peppers in 1/2 cup hot water for 5 to 10 minutes. Stir in remaining ingredients, except last 1 cup water. Gradually add water. Heat through, stirring occasionally and serve over cooked pasta. This can be thinned with more water if you wish.

Mexican Sauce (makes about 1 cup)

1 Tbs. dried onions
1 cup water + 1/4 cup hot water
1 Tbs. dried green and red peppers
dash of cayenne or hot sauce

3 Tbs. tomato base
1/2 tsp. chili powder
cumin to taste

Rehydrate onions and peppers in 1/4 cup hot water for 5-10 minutes. Add remaining ingredients and heat through, stirring occasionally. Serve with Bean and Cheese Enchiladas, Chili Rellenos, or to give a Mexican flavor to rice, pastas, etc. Our taste testers loved it on pizza!

QUICK BREADS

Basic Quick Bread

2/3 cup whole wheat flour
2/3 cup white flour
1 1/2 tsp. baking powder
1/2 tsp. salt

2 heaping Tbs. margarine
1/3 cup powdered milk
1 1/2 cups water

Mix all ingredients. Pour into a fry pan, cover and bake about 15 minutes or until done. Use a twiggy fire.

Variations:
1. Fruit and Nut Quick Bread—make basic recipe above and add 2 Tbs. brown sugar and 1/2 cup chopped fruits and/or nuts of your choice. Bake as above.

2. Italian Quick Bread—to the basic quick bread recipe add 1 tsp. garlic powder, 1 tsp. crushed oregano, 2 tsp. vinegar (optional), 3 Tbs. Parmesan, and 1 Tbs. dried onion (rehydrated in hot water, then drained). Mix all ingredients together and bake as above.

Cornbread

1 cup cornmeal
1/2 cup whole wheat flour
1/3 cup white flour
3 Tbs. honey or brown sugar
1/2 tsp. vanilla

1 Tbs. baking powder
1 tsp. salt
2/3 cup powdered milk
1 1/2 cups water

Mix together dry ingredients. Gradually add water, vanilla and honey, stirring well. Pour into a *greased* fry pan, cover and bake using a twiggy fire for about 15 minutes or until done.

Variation: For Mexican Cornbread use the above recipe with the following changes: reduce honey or sugar to 1 1/2 Tbs. and add 1 cup jack cheese (crumbled or diced small), 1/8 tsp. Tabasco, 1 tsp. cumin, 1/4 tsp. cayenne, and 2 - 3 Tbs. dried peppers (rehydrated in hot water, then drained). Bake as above.

Banana Bread

1/3 cup whole wheat flour
2/3 cup white flour
1 cup banana chips, crushed
1 1/2 tsp. baking powder
1/2 tsp. salt
1/4 cup margarine, melted
1/4 tsp. cinnamon (or apple pie spice mix)

1/3 cup powdered milk
3 Tbs. brown sugar
1 Tbs. powdered egg
2/3 cup chopped walnuts
3/4 - 1 1/4 cup water

Combine all dry ingredients, including nuts and banana chips; mix. Stir in melted margarine and add water gradually to form a pancake-type batter. Pour into fry pan, cover and bake using a twiggy fire for 15 to 25 minutes or until done.

Peanut Butter-Banana Bread

1/2 cup peanut butter
2 heaping Tbs. margarine, melted
1 cup banana chips, crushed
1 cup whole wheat flour
1/2 tsp. salt
2 cups water

1/2 cup honey
2 Tbs. powdered egg
1 cup white flour
1 1/2 tsp. baking powder
3/4 cup powdered milk

Mix peanut butter, honey and margarine. Blend dry ingredients. Add with water to peanut butter mixture and stir well. Bake in covered fry pan approximately 25 minutes, using a twiggy fire.

Variations: to either banana bread recipe add 1/2 cup of one of the following: chopped peanuts or walnuts, coconut, chopped dried fruits, carob or other flavored chips, or try a mix of several.

YEAST BREADS

Yeast are tiny one-cell organisms that are dormant until combined with warm water and sugar or starch. Too hot water kills the yeast; too cold will not activate it. As the yeast grow and multiply, carbon dioxide gas is given off.

Flour, salt, water and yeast are the basics of bread to which other ingredients are added for variety. Wheat flour is best because it is high in gluten, fibers which become elastic when kneaded and hold the gas pockets created by the yeast. Other flours (graham, buckwheat, etc.) are tasty but require more skill in handling. We recommend making basic breads which usually work well even under less than ideal conditions.

Basic Bread

1 level Tbs. yeast
2 Tbs. margarine or oil (optional)
1 1/2 cups lukewarm water (drop a few drops
*   by spoon onto you wrist to test the temperature)*
3-3 1/2 cups flour (1/3 whole wheat, 2/3 white is good)

2 tsp. salt
2 Tbs. sugar

Dissolve yeast in lukewarm water with sugar, salt, and oil. Let set about 5 minutes in warm spot until it froths. (Try putting it in a NOLS mug and capping it. When frothed it bubbles through the hole a little). Add half the flour and beat vigorously 2-3 minutes to develop gluten; the wet batter smooths out and starts to get a little "stringy". Add remaining flour and margarine to get a thick dough. Flour your hands and knead the bread on a floured fry pan, flat rock or ensolite pad. Knead with the heels of your hands about 8 minutes, folding and turning to knead all parts evenly. Add more flour when dough becomes too sticky to handle. The dough will be silky and springy when done.

Shape into a loaf and place in well oiled pot or fry pan. Press the dough out to touch edges and grease top of the loaf. Cover and set in a warm place to rise for about an hour, or until doubled in size. If it's very cold outside, let it rise by placing it on top of a pan of boiling water with a cover over it. Once risen, bake the bread 30-50 minutes. When done, bread will be golden brown and will have a hollow sound when thumped. Take out of pan and cool with good circulation 5-10 minutes before cutting.

Variation: Pinch off pieces of dough and bake as large rolls rather than a loaf.

Beefy Onion-Cheese Bread

Add to basic recipe:

1 Tbs. beef base instead of salt
1-2 Tbs. rehydrated onions (using onion water as part of the recipe
*   water)*
1 cup crumbled or diced cheese
(Can be made without cheese, but increase onions to 3 Tbs.)

Follow above directions for preparation and baking.

Cinnamon-Raisin Yeast Bread

Follow basic yeast bread recipe, adding 1/2 cup raisins, 2 tsp. cinnamon and 1/2 cup sugar to the yeast water.

Nut Fruit Yeast Bread

Add 1 cup chopped fruit, nuts and seeds to the basic recipe.

Oatmeal or Cereal Yeast Bread

Replace 1 cup of wheat flour with 1 cup of oatmeal (or try 1 cup cooked bulgar to get a wheatberry bread).

Leftovers Bread

1 cup cooked leftovers (rice, cereals, bulgar, lentils, beans, potatoes or
*   cous-cous, etc.)*

1 1/2 cups whole wheat flour	*1/2 Tbs. salt*
1 1/2 cups white flour	*2 Tbs. powdered milk*
(can use all of one type if desired)	*2 Tbs. yeast*
1 cup warm water	*1 Tbs. brown sugar or honey*
3 Tbs. margarine or oil	*2 Tbs. powdered egg*

In a bowl add water, yeast, sugar and margarine. Set aside for 5 minutes to activate yeast. In another bowl mix together half the flour with the other dry ingredients. Add in the leftovers, stir, then add in the yeast mixture, stirring well. Work the remaining flour in as you're kneading the dough. It should have a smooth elastic consistency. Knead 5 minutes. You can cover this with a damp cloth and let sit in the sun 45 minutes to double in size, then punch down and form a loaf and let rise again for about 20 minutes in a greased pan, or you can let it rise only once in a greased pan. (Letting dough rise twice makes for a lighter bread.) Bake on stove over low heat, using a twiggy fire for 20-35 minutes or until done. It should have a moist, chewy consistency.

Variation: Experiment with spices or other flavorings. This bread may pick up a lot of flavor from the seasonings used in the leftovers.

Fry Bread (serves 2*)

1 3/4 - 2 cups flour (a mix of white and whole wheat is good)

2 tsp. yeast	*3/4 cup warm water*
1 tsp. salt	*1 tsp. sugar*
oil for frying	

*If you double this recipe, cook half at a time.

Mix all ingredients except flour. Let stand 5 minutes. Add flour and knead until smooth. Let rise. (To use next morning, put dough into plastic bag, squeezing out air, tie knot in bag; put into another bag left untied. Sleep with dough overnight to keep it warm.)

Heat oil in fry pan. Flatten dough into a fat tortilla 1/2 inch thick. Fry bread on both sides. Serve with a spread of honey/brown sugar, margarine and cinnamon. How much oil you use for frying determines the crust and texture of this bread. Real fry bread uses a lot of oil, but it is not necessary and cuts down on fat calories to just oil the pan.

Indian Fry Bread

Mix bread as above and use immediately without allowing it to rise.

Variation: Add up to 2 cups leftover cooked pinto beans and fry as above.

BISCUITS

Basic Biscuits (makes 10-12 biscuits)

2 cups baking mix (see recipe index)   1/2 to 3/4 cup water
4 Tbs. margarine

Cut margarine into baking mix using spoon edges. Add enough water to form a stiff dough. Knead in bowl about a dozen times. Pinch off enough dough for desired size biscuit; pat into shape. Bake in covered fry pan, using a twiggy fire, for about 15-20 minutes or until done. As an alternative to baking, fry in melted margarine until both sides are browned. Cover and cook on low heat about 8-10 minutes. Good served with margarine and a white sauce.

Variation: Mix together 1 Tbs. margarine, 1 Tbs. brown sugar and 1/3 cup chopped mixed fruits and nuts and insert into biscuits using method described in recipe below.

Cheesy Biscuits (makes 10-12 biscuits)

Follow the basic recipe and add 1/2 tsp. garlic powder and some rehydrated onions to dough. Form into balls and pull apart into halves. Add a piece of cheese and pinch halves back together. Bake as above.

Chicken Bisketts

1 1/2 cups flour   1 - 2 tsp. chicken base
1/4 cup cornmeal   2 Tbs. margarine
1 tsp. baking powder
1 - 2 tsp. dried onions rehydrated in 1/2 cup water or milk

Mix dry ingredients; cut in margarine. Stir in water (with onions) to form a dough. Pinch off pieces and make thin cakes. Roll in cornmeal. Oil and heat a fry pan. Bake, covered, for about 20 minutes.

MUFFINS

Whole Wheat-Cornmeal Cheese Muffins

1 cup whole wheat flour
1/2 cup cornmeal
1/2 cup crumbled or cubed cheddar
1 heaping Tbs. powdered milk
1/4 cup cheese powder (very optional)

1 heaping Tbs. powdered egg
1 1/2 tsp. baking powder
3/4 - 1 cup water

Mix all dry ingredients. Add water gradually, stirring to form a slightly sticky dough. Mix in the cheese. Spoon mixture onto hot oiled pan. Cover and cook over medium heat until top is fairly set then flip and finish cooking. Takes about 20-25 minutes. Good trail food.

Variation: Omit cheese and add raisins and nuts (about 1/2 cup total), vanilla, cinnamon and 1 Tbs. brown sugar for a sweet muffin. Serve with honey, peanut butter or margarine.

Oat Stones (makes 6-8 large scones)

An oatmeal scone with substance that is great plain or with honey, peanut butter, wild berry jam or cheese—an excellent bread with soups or stews and a good trail food.

2 cups oatmeal
1/4 cup honey or brown sugar
1 1/2 tsp. baking powder
pinch of salt (allows recipe to use less sweetener)
1/2 tsp. vanilla (omit for a less sweet taste)

2 cups white flour
1/2 cup margarine
water

Melt margarine in a pot and stir in oatmeal to soak it up. Add baking powder, salt and honey; mix thoroughly. Add water and flour alternately until mixture is neither too sticky nor too dry to hold together well. Form patties about 4" by 3/4" thick. These can be cooked by frying on both sides until done, but they come out much lighter, with better flavor when baked with a twiggy fire for about 20-25 minutes or until cooked through.

Variation: Cook fruit such as dates in water until mushy. Add sugar to taste and some flour to soak up water and use as a filling. Place spoonful between two thin patties, seal edges and bake. Makes a giant Fig Newton-type pastry.

Crowns a la Sierra (makes 8-10)

This recipe is an instant hit!

2 cups baking mix (see recipe index)
3 heaping Tbs. margarine   *1/2 to 3/4 cup water*
1/2 cup brown sugar   *filling (see below)*
1 tsp. apple pie spice mix or 1/2 - 1 tsp. cinnamon

Mix dry ingredients. Cut in margarine. Add water to make a stiff dough. Pinch off dough and roll into balls. Bake in fry pan, using twiggy fire, for 5 minutes, then indent middle with a spoon and continue baking until brown, about 15-20 minutes more. Just before serving, fill depression in center with the following filling mix:

3 Tbs. honey or brown sugar (with sugar add 1 Tbs. water)
1/2 cup nuts and chopped fruit (good combo is raisins, chopped walnuts
    and chopped apricots)
1 heaping Tbs. Margarine
dash of salt
1/2 tsp. either cinnamon or apple pie spice mix

Mix together and cook over low heat a few minutes until smooth.

SPECIALTIES

Corn Tortillas (makes 12)

2 cups cornmeal   *1/2 tsp. salt*
1/2 cup whole wheat flour   *2/3 - 1 cup water*

Mix dry ingredients. Add in water until you get a smooth dough that easily forms a ball. Should not be sticky or too dry to hold its shape. Knead for about 5 minutes. Cover and let sit 15 minutes. Divide into 12 balls. Place one ball at a time in the middle of a plastic bag and roll into a 5-6" circle. Cook quickly on both sides in a hot, *unoiled* fry pan.

Flour Tortillas (makes 12)

3 cups white flour   *1/2 cup warm water*
1/4 tsp. salt   *1/4 cup margarine*
1 tsp. baking powder (optional—using makes a puffier tortilla)

Mix dry ingredients together. Cut in margarine, using two knives or spoon edges. Add water and mix well with your hands. Proceed as in Corn Tortillas above.

Uses for Tortillas
1. Melt cheese on top for quesadillas; serve with picante or hot sauce.
2. Add margarine, hot sauce and cheese to warmed up leftover grains such as rice or cous-cous and roll up in a tortilla.
3. Heat oil in fry pan, quickly fry a flour tortilla in the hot oil (it will puff up) and serve with stewed apples or other fruit or sprinkle with cinnamon and sugar. Can top this with cheese too.
4. Stuff tortillas with spicy cooked beans and cheese, roll up and place in fry pan, cover with Mexican sauce, cook (covered) until heated through.
5. Use as a bread for any sandwich making.
6. Spread with Power Peanut Butter (see recipe index) and raisins and roll up.
7. Break cooked tortillas into large pieces, fry in hot oil, melt cheese on top and serve with picante for Nachos.

Chappaties (makes 4 5" flat breads)

1/2 cup flour (whole wheat is more authentic, white is okay too)
1/2 cup cornmeal   *1/2 cup water*
pinch of salt   *margarine for frying*

Toppings: sliced cheese, bacon bits, chopped wild onions, cayenne or Tabasco

Mix all ingredients except margarine. Form into very thin patties and fry in lightly greased pan until golden brown. After they are turned, add sliced cheese or whatever other toppings you wish; cover pan to help cheese melt.

Variation: Combine 1 cup whole wheat flour, 1 Tbs. margarine, 1/4 tsp. salt, 1/4 cup water. Proceed as for making Chappaties.

Empanadas (makes 10-12 Mexican Turnovers)

2 cups flour   *2 tsp. baking powder*
1/3 - 1/2 cup reconstituted milk   *1/2 cup margarine*
1 tsp. salt (use only 1/4 tsp. if you fry in margarine rather than oil)
margarine or oil for frying   *Filling (see below)*

Mix flour, baking powder and salt, if used. Cut in 1/2 cup margarine. Add milk to form a pie crust dough. Roll out thin and cut in 4" circles. On one half of each circle place a small spoonful of filling. Seal other half over. Use a little powdered egg mixed with water to seal turnovers. Heat margarine or oil in fry pan. Fry empanadas on both sides until dough is cooked.

Fillings for Empanadas:
1 Mixture of brown sugar and margarine.
2. Mixture of chopped dried apples and raisins (let sit in hot water a while then drain), add 1 Tbs. margarine, 2 Tbs. chopped nuts and 1 Tbs. flour if seems too juicy.
3. Mixture of canned chicken, chopped cheese and curry powder.

Yeast Cinnamon Rolls
An impressive speciality at home or on the trail.

1 basic bread dough recipe   *1/2 - 1 cup brown sugar*
1 Tbs. cinnamon   *4 Tbs. margarine*
1/2 cup each, nuts and raisins (optional but wonderful)

Mix up basic bread recipe and roll out into a large rectangle 1/2 inch thick. Spread with margarine. Sprinkle with cinnamon, sugar, nuts and raisins. Roll up jelly roll style, pinching dough closed so sugar doesn't fall out. Slice roll into 1 inch slices and place in pan. Cover and bake using a twiggy fire, for 25 to 35 minutes or until done. (You can pinch underside of rolls together before putting into pan to prevent hot sugar from leaking out and scorching, however, with good baking techniques that leakage can be good, forming a delicious glaze.)

Variation: Substitute apple cider mix powder for sugar and cinnamon.

Quick Cinnamon Rolls
3 cups baking mix   *3 Tbs. margarine*
1 - 1 1/2 cups water   *1/2 cup brown sugar*
3/4 Tbs. cinnamon   *extra flour for rolling*
1/4 cup each, raisins and nuts

Mix together baking mix and water. Roll out on floured surface—adding more flour to make less sticky if necessary. Follow procedure for yeast cinnamon rolls. Bake for 15-25 minutes.

10,000 STEPS TO PERFECT CINNAMON ROLLS

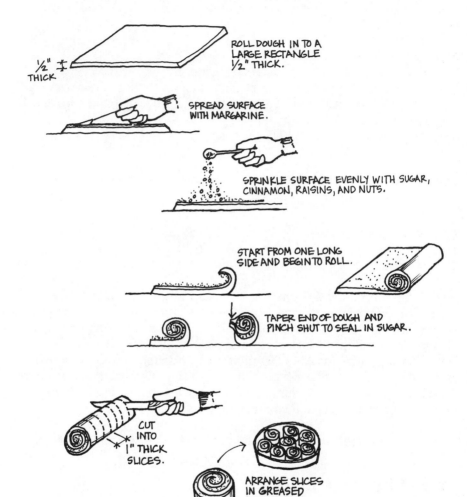

ROLL DOUGH INTO A LARGE RECTANGLE 1/2" THICK.

1/2" THICK

SPREAD SURFACE WITH MARGARINE.

SPRINKLE SURFACE EVENLY WITH SUGAR, CINNAMON, RAISINS, AND NUTS.

START FROM ONE LONG SIDE AND BEGIN TO ROLL.

TAPER END OF DOUGH AND PINCH SHUT TO SEAL IN SUGAR.

CUT INTO 1" THICK SLICES.

ARRANGE SLICES IN GREASED BAKING PAN.

AND BAKE!

BUILD TWIGGY FIRE OR USE COALS ON TOP.

"PERFECT!"

PLACE ON COALS OR STOVE AND DILIGENTLY FOLLOW THE "ROUND THE CLOCK" METHOD FOR BAKING!

SPREADABLES

All the following are good in hot cereal, on crackers, bagels, biscuits, pancakes, bread and muffins.

Power Peanut Butter Spread (makes about 1 cup)

1/2 cup peanut butter   *1/4 cup margarine*
1/4 cup honey   *1/3 cup powdered milk*

Carefully melt peanut butter, honey and margarine in a pot. Stir in powdered milk.

Variations: Add sunflower seeds, chopped nuts, raisins, chopped dried fruit.

Wild Berry Jam

2 cups berries
1/2 - 1 cup brown sugar
1 - 2 Tbs. flour to thicken if desired

Wash berries and crush them. Measure out 2 cups and put into pan. Bring to a boil. Add sugar and flour. Cook rapidly until thick. Stir frequently to prevent burning.

Cinnamon-Honey "Butter"

Mix 1/4 cup margarine with 1 Tbs. honey and 1/4 tsp. cinnamon.

DESSERTS AND SNACKS

Basic Cake Recipe (for a 10 inch fry pan)

1 1/2 cups baking mix (see recipe index)
1/2 cup flour
4 Tbs. brown sugar or honey
2 - 3 Tbs. margarine, melted
1 tsp. vanilla
about 1 1/2 cups cold water (or more—for a pourable batter)

1/2 cup powdered milk
pinch of salt
2 level Tbs. powdered egg

Mix all dry ingredients. Add liquid ingredients and mix until lumps are out. Pour into greased, floured fry pan. Cover and bake, using a twiggy fire, 15-25 minutes, or until done. Loosen and remove from pan. Cool and frost or try lemon Jell-O or cream cake variations.

Variations:
1. Chocolate: Use 3/4 cup cocoa mix to replace powdered milk.
2. Cinnamon-Raisin: Add 1/2 cup softened, drained raisins and 1 tsp. cinnamon or apple pie spice mix.
3. Peanut: Omit salt, add 1/2 cup crushed peanuts and 1/2 cup extra sugar.
4. Fruit Cake: Use 1/2 cup fruit drink crystals in place of sugar.
5. Lemon Jello Cake: Make plain cake, remove from pan, poke holes in top with fork or very small twig; dissolve 3 Tbs. lemon Jell-O powder in 1/2 cup boiling water. Spoon over top of cake and let sit 10 minutes before serving.
6. Cream Cake: Make plain cake, remove from pan, cool 10 minutes. Cut cake in half horizontally. Mix up a thick pudding, using less milk, and fill between layers. Frost with butterscotch or chocolate frosting.

Lucy Smith's Apple Pie Cake (10 inch pan cake)

1 cup dried apples, chopped
2 cups baking mix (see recipe index)
1/2 cup raisins (optional)
1 tsp. apple pie spice mix or cinnamon
2 - 3 Tbs. melted margarine
1/4 cup apple cider mix or 4 Tbs. brown sugar or honey
1 1/4 - 1 1/2 cups water (use drained fruit water in this)
crushed sesame-honey candies for topping (optional)

1/2 cup powdered milk
2 Tbs. powdered egg
pinch of salt
water for cooking fruit
1 tsp. vanilla

Put apples, raisins, and apple pie spice or cinnamon in pan with water to cover. Bring to boil, simmer 10 minutes. Cool. Mix all dry ingredients. Drain water off fruit and add to the 1 1/4 - 1 1/2 cups water needed. Add this, vanilla, and margarine to dry ingredients. Stir well. Mix in drained fruit. Pour into greased and floured 10-inch fry pan. Cover and bake about 25 minutes or until done, using a twiggy fire. If you are using crushed candy topping, sprinkle it on cake halfway through baking time.

Pineapple Upside Down Cake

Make up Basic Cake batter recipe. Melt 2 Tbs. margarine in 10 inch fry pan. Mix in 3 - 4 Tbs. brown sugar and spread over bottom of pan. Place pineapple rings or pieces on sugar mixture. Pour batter over pineapple. Bake, using a twiggy fire, for 15-25 minutes.

Coffee Cake (for a 10-inch fry pan)

1 3/4 cup flour
2 tsp. baking powder
1/2 tsp. salt
4 Tbs. margarine, melted
1 tsp. vanilla

1/2 cup brown sugar
1 Tbs. powdered egg
1/3 cup powdered milk
1/2 cup water

Grease and flour pan. Mix dry ingredients; add liquids and stir. Bake 12-18 minutes, using a twiggy fire. Serve with stewed spiced apples or wild berry sauce poured over each serving. Also good plain or with honey-cinnamon butter.

Streussel Coffee Cake

Make above recipe. Sprinkle with a topping made from 5 Tbs. brown sugar, 1/3 cup oatmeal, 4 Tbs. margarine and 1 tsp. cinnamon mixed well together. Bake, using a twiggy fire, for 15-25 minutes.

Blueberry Cake

Cook one cup fresh berries with 1 Tbs. sugar or honey, 2 Tbs. margarine, 2 Tbs. flour and about 3/4 cup water. It should be quite thick. Spread over Basic Coffee Cake batter and bake as above.

Gingerbread Coffee Cake

Make Basic recipe except use 1 cup flour and 1 cup gingerbread mix; reduce sugar to 1/4 - 1/3 cup, reduce baking powder to 1 tsp., reduce salt to 1/4 tsp. Bake as above.

Cheesecake

Crust:

3 Tbs. margarine   1 Tbs. brown sugar
1 1/2 cups Grapenuts   3 - 4 Tbs. water

Melt margarine and sugar in fry pan. Add Grapenuts and stir for 2-3 minutes. Add water and stir another minute. Remove from heat. Use back of spoon to press Grapenuts evenly over bottom and 1 inch up the sides of the pan. Set aside to cool.

Filling:

2 cups cheesecake mix (3/4 lb.)   6 Tbs. powdered milk
1 tsp. vanilla (optional)   2 - 2 1/2 cups water

Add water slowly to dry ingredients, blending to avoid lumps. Pour into cooled crust. Put in cool place to set up.

Optional Topping:
Drain some liquid from canned blueberries and mix 1 - 1 1/2 Tbs. flour into it. Pour berries and remaining juice into pot. Heat; stir in flour mixture. Cook until thick, stirring frequently. Cool. Pour over set cheesecake.

Variation: Drain liquid from berries and just spoon some berries over each serving, or if fresh berries are available make topping used for Blueberry Cake.

Chocolate Cheesecake

Proceed as above but add 1/3 cup cocoa mix to filling. Add carob chips if desired. Omit blueberry topping.

Scrambled Brownies or Gingerbread

2 cups brownie mix or gingerbread mix
6 Tbs. water (add more if batter is dry)

Mix together. Spread in oiled fry pan. Cover and cook on low heat about 15 minutes until product is done on top. Scrape out of pan with a spatula. Let sit a few minutes before eating so it can stiffen up. This is an alternative to baking with a twiggy fire. The end product is chewy, gooey!

Fruit Bars

Crust:
1 cup flour (mix white and whole wheat)
1 cup oatmeal
1/4 tsp. salt
6 - 8 Tbs. margarine

1/2 tsp. baking powder
4 Tbs. brown sugar

Mix together with fingers and pat into bottom of fry pan.

Filling:
1 cup chopped dates (or combination of dried fruit)
2 Tbs. sugar or honey　　　　*1/3 cup water*

Combine all ingredients in a pan; simmer until liquid is gone. Pour onto crust and spread. Sprinkle Grapenuts or granola over top. Bake, using a twiggy fire, for 20-25 minutes.

Variation: For bottom crust make up Basic Cookie recipe (see recipe index) and spread into bottom of pan. Follow remaining instructions above.

Apple Crisp

1 1/2 cup dried apples,chopped　　*1/2 cup raisins*
1/2 tsp. cinnamon or apple pie spice mix
hot water to just cover fruit in pot　*1/4 tsp. salt*
1/2 cup chopped walnuts or almonds

Combine all ingredients except nuts in a pot and let soak until fruit rehydrates—about 15 minutes. Meanwhile combine the following:

1/4 - 1/2 cup oatmeal　　*3 Tbs. brown sugar*
3 Tbs. flour　　*pinch of salt*
4 heaping Tbs. margarine

Mix together with hands to a crumbly consistency. Grease a fry pan. Add nuts to fruit mixture and pour into pan. (If there is a lot of liquid, stir in 1 Tbs. flour.) Cover with oatmeal mix. Bake, using a twiggy fire, for about 15 minutes until heated through and browned on top.

Apple Strudel

2 cups flour　　*1 tsp. baking powder*
1/4 tsp. salt　　*2 Tbs. melted margarine*
3/4 cup milk (5 Tbs. powdered milk and water to make 3/4 cup)

Mix dry ingredients. Add milk and margarine to make a dough. Roll out to a rectangle.

Filling:
2 cups dried apples
1/2 cup brown sugar or 1/3 cup honey
1 tsp. cinnamon or apple pie spice mix
1 - 2 Tbs. flour

1/2 cup chopped nuts
water to cover

Combine all ingredients in a pan, except flour, and bring to a boil. Add flour to 2 Tbs. of hot liquid, mix and return to pot. Cook gently until apples are tender. Cool. Brush dough with margarine. Spread on filling; roll; seal ends and bake, using a twiggy fire, about 15-25 minutes or until crust is done. (Can brush the top of the dough with margarine before baking.)

Fruit Cobbler

1 cup water + 1/2 cup
2 Tbs. brown sugar
1 tsp. cinnamon
1/2 cup flour
1/4 cup powdered milk
1 cup baking mix cut with 1 Tbs. margarine
1 - 1 1/2 cup dried fruit (mixed fruit works well)

1 heaping Tbs. margarine
pinch of salt
1/4 cup chopped walnuts
3/4 cup water

Put 1 cup water, fruit, nuts, salt, 1 Tbs. margarine, brown sugar, cinnamon into a pan and bring to a boil. Cook for several minutes to rehydrate, then add 1/2 cup water more. Mix remaining ingredients together to form a stiff dough. Drop by spoonfuls onto gently boiling fruit. Cover and steam about 10 minutes until pastry dumplings are done.

FROSTINGS

Quick Topping

Sprinkle 2 Tbs. brown sugar, 1/4 tsp. cinnamon and 2 Tbs. margarine on top of a cake when done, put lid back on and bake for a few more minutes until margarine melts.

Chocolate Frosting

4 Tbs. margarine, melted
1/4 - 1/2 cup brown sugar
2 Tbs. water (or coffee for mocha)

1/2 cup cocoa mix

Combine all ingredients and cook on low heat, stirring vigorously. Add nuts, fruit or coconut for variety. Pour over cake.

Butterscotch Frosting

4 Tbs. margarine, melted
1/2 cup brown sugar

2 Tbs. water
4 Tbs. powdered milk

Mix as above for chocolate frosting. If it seems granular, add another Tbs. water and stir until it becomes more creamy.

Sesame-Honey Topping

Crush sesame-honey candies and sprinkle over top of cake halfway through baking time.

Orange-Coconut Frosting

1/2 orange peel, diced fine
1/2 cup orange fruit crystals
1/3 cup brown sugar
3 Tbs. water

4 Tbs. margarine
3 Tbs. powdered milk
1/4 cup coconut

Heat margarine, sugar, fruit crystals, coconut and peel over moderate heat, stirring. Mix water and milk and add to mixture after margarine melts. Simmer about 5 minutes until it thickens. Add more water if too thick. Take off heat, let set 1 minute, spread on cake.

Basic Cookies (9 3" cookies)

1/2 cup brown sugar
1/4 cup margarine
1/4 cup powdered milk
3 Tbs. water

3/4 cup baking mix
1/2 cup white flour
1/8 tsp. salt

Cream sugar and margarine together. Mix milk powder and water and add to sugar mixture. Combine flour, salt and baking mix and add to other ingredients, working it into a stiff dough. Divide into nine pieces. Flatten and bake for about 10 minutes, using a twiggy fire.

Variations:

1. Cinnamon: Sprinkle mixture of 1 1/2 Tbs. brown sugar and 1/2 tsp. cinnamon over cookies before baking.
2. Fruit and Nut: Mix 1/2 cup (total) of your choice of fruit, nuts and seeds into dough. Try raisins with walnuts, apricots with almonds, pineapple and sunflower seeds.

3. Carob/Chocolate Chip: Add 1 tsp. vanilla, 1/3 cup carob or chocolate chips, and 1/4 cup chopped walnuts.
4. Peanut Butter: Omit salt, add 4 Tbs. peanut butter, 2 Tbs more flour and 1/4 cup chopped peanuts.
5. Chocolate: Add 1/2 cup cocoa and 4 Tbs. water instead of powdered milk mixture.

Nitty Gritty Cornmeal Cookies (about 12-15 2 1/2" cookies)

1/2 cup margarine
1/2 - 1 tsp. vanilla
2/3 cup flour + 1 Tbs.

6 Tbs. brown sugar
1/3 cup cornmeal
extra cornmeal for rolling
pinch of salt

Combine margarine and brown sugar. Add other ingredients to form a stiff dough. Roll 1 Tbs. dough into a ball. Roll it in the extra cornmeal. Flatten to 1/4 inch thickness. Bake using a twiggy fire, for 8-10 minutes or until done. Cool for a moment before removing from pan.

Granola Chewies (makes about 12 3" cookies or 2 pan-size ones)

1 cup granola
1/2 cup margarine
1/2 tsp. salt
1/2 cup brown sugar (or 6 Tbs. sugar + 2 Tbs. honey)
2 Tbs. powdered egg into 2 Tbs. water

3/4 cup flour
1/2 tsp. baking powder
1/2 tsp. vanilla

Mix together and drop by spoonfuls onto a frying pan. Cover and bake, using a twiggy fire, for 8-10 minutes. Cookies will set up as they cool.

Oatmeal Crackers (makes 24-30 1 1/2" squares)

1/4 cup margarine
1/4 cup brown sugar
1/4 - 1/2 tsp. vanilla
3 Tbs. powdered milk
4 Tbs. water

1 cup oatmeal
1 cup + 2 Tbs. flour
3/4 tsp. baking powder
pinch of salt

Mix milk powder and water; add to creamed margarine and brown sugar. Add vanilla and stir in oatmeal. Mix dry ingredients together and add to mixture. Dough should hold together but not be sticky. Add a bit more milk or flour if needed to reach proper consistency. Roll half the dough as thin as possible and cut into 1-2 inch squares. Put crackers into a heated, slightly oiled fry pan. Cook, covered for 6-8 minutes, using a twiggy fire, or fry on both sides. Repeat with remaining dough. Good plain, with cheese, with berry jam or peanut butter spread.

Almond Sandies (makes 20-24 cookies)

A good way to use up extra margarine, flour, and nuts.

1 1/2 cups margarine   *3/4 cup brown sugar*
2/3 cup finely chopped almonds   *1 tsp. vanilla*
3 cups flour (white or mostly white works best)

Mix together into a dough with your hands. Break off spoon-size pieces. Roll into a ball and flatten. Fry in a heated, *dry* pan for about 4 minutes per side, or bake in a covered pan, using a twiggy fire, for about 8-10 minutes. Baked version is more cookie-like. Fried version should sit a few minutes after cooking to set up.

No-Bake Eskimo Cookies (about 16 cookies)

6 Tbs. margarine   *3 Tbs. cocoa mix*
6 Tbs. brown sugar   *1/2 tsp. vanilla*
1 cup oatmeal   *1/2 Tbs. water*

Mix all ingredients together. Form into walnut-sized balls. Eat immediately or let sit in a cool place.

Variation: Roll in a combination of 1 Tbs. powdered milk and 1 Tbs. brown sugar, or in coconut.

No-Bake Powerhouse Cookies (makes 20-24 cookies)

Our taste-testers loved these!

1 cup brown sugar   *1 cup peanut butter*
1/4 cup margarine   *1/2 tsp. vanilla*
3 Tbs. powdered milk   *1 cup oatmeal*
4 Tbs. water   *1/4 cup carob chips*
1/2 cup Spanish (or blanched) peanuts

Mix sugar, margarine, powdered milk and water in a pan. Bring to a boil. Reduce heat and boil 3 minutes. Stir constantly to prevent scorching. Remove from heat and stir in remaining ingredients. Drop by spoonfuls onto a flat surface such as pan lids. Let sit for about 10 minutes to set up. In hot weather, they might not set up as well.

Chewy Fudge No-Bake Cookies

1 cup brown sugar   *1 1/2 cups oatmeal*
5 Tbs. margarine   *1/4 cup walnuts or almonds*
1/4 cup cocoa mix   *1/2 tsp. vanilla*
3 Tbs. powdered milk   *3 Tbs. water*

Mix sugar, margarine, cocoa and milk (made from the milk powder and water) together in a pan. Follow same cooking procedures as in No-Bake Powerhouse Cookies.

PIES

Easy Crust (for a 10-inch pan)

1/4 tsp. salt

4 Tbs. margarine

2/3 - 1 cup flour

2 Tbs. brown sugar

Melt margarine and mix in other ingredients until crust is consistency of a graham cracker crust—not greasy but a bit dry. Pat into bottom of a frying pan and bake 5-10 minutes or until golden brown. Cool and add a cooked filling or an instant pudding.

Roll Crust (for a 10-inch pan)

Make the crust shown in the Quiche Moraine recipe (see recipe index). Bake for 5-10 minutes and add a cooked filling or instant pudding. Or add uncooked filling and bake filling and crust at same time until crust is browned and filling is cooked.

Fruit Pie Filling

1 1/2 cups dried fruit

2 cups water

2-3 Tbs. flour

1 tsp. cinnamon or apple pie spice mix

1/2 - 2/3 cup sugar (to taste, depending on fruit used)

1/2 cup chopped nuts

2 Tbs. margarine

pinch of salt

Simmer fruit in water until hydrated. Drain off all juice but about 1/2 cup. Save drained juice. Add margarine, salt, sugar and spice to fruit. Stir well. Mix flour with drained-off juice (about 1/3 cup) and stir into fruit. Add nuts. Simmer, stirring often until thickened. Pour into an already baked crust and allow to set up. Can garnish with granola, coconut, etc.

Variation: This can be make with fresh fruit or berries. Increase the amount of fruit and decrease the water. Adjust with your thickener.

Rice Pudding (serves 3-4)

2 cups cooked brown or white rice

1/2 cup raisins

6 Tbs. brown sugar or honey

2 fresh eggs, beaten, or 1 1/2 Tbs. powdered egg*

dash of apple pie spice mix or nutmeg

1/2 - 1 1/2 tsp. vanilla (depending on strength)

1 1/3 cup water

2/3 cup powdered milk

1/2 tsp. cinnamon

*If using powdered egg, mix 1 1/2 Tbs. flour with egg and add some water. Pour mixture into rice and cook.

Combine all except vanilla. Cook over low heat, stirring constantly, until thickened—about 10-15 minutes. DO NOT BOIL. Stir in vanilla.

Variation: Stir in 1/4 - 1/2 cup peanut butter as it cooks.

Ian's Vanilla Ice Cream

Fill a NOLS mug with fresh snow (1 1/2 cup). Stir in 2 Tbs. powdered milk, 1 Tbs. brown sugar and 1/2 - 1 tsp. vanilla. Stir until creamy.

Variations:
1. Chocolate: Omit brown sugar and add 2 Tbs. cocoa mix.
2. Fruit: Omit sugar and vanilla, add 1 Tbs. lemon or orange fruit crystals—it's tangier without the powdered milk.
3. Apple: Omit sugar and vanilla, add 1 Tbs. apple cider mix and a dash of cinnamon.
4. Cheesecake: Omit sugar and vanilla and add 1-2 Tbs. cheesecake mix.

Peanut Brittle/Peanut Popcorn

2 Tbs. margarine *pinch of salt*
1/2 - 1 cup brown sugar
1 cup peanuts or popcorn

Melt margarine. Dissolve sugar in it, stirring constantly while cooking. When a small spoonful of the hot sugar mixture forms a ball on being dropped into cold water, it is done. Add salt and peanuts or popcorn; stir; cool immediately by placing pan in snow or cold water.

Caramels/Chocolate Caramels

3 Tbs. margarine *1/2 cup powdered milk*
1 cup brown sugar *3 Tbs. water*
2 Tbs. cocoa mix (for chocolate version)
1 cup nuts, seeds or popcorn

Mix water into powdered milk and cocoa. Follow directions for peanut brittle, adding milk mixture after sugar has dissolved and continuing to cook. If mixture is granular, add 1 - 2 Tbs. water and it will smooth out. You can drop spoonfuls onto a clean rock or into snow and let them set up.

Peanut Butter Delights (a complete protein)

1/2 cup sesame or raw sunflower seeds   *2 - 3 heaping Tbs. honey*
1 heaping Tbs. powdered milk   *2 heaping Tbs. peanut butter*
coconut or crushed sesame-honey candies

Mix together. Add more powdered milk if sticky. It should form a fairly stiff dough. Make into balls and roll in coconut or crushed sesame-honey candies. Ready to eat.

Stuffed Dates (makes 12)

12 dates   *1 Tbs. brown sugar*
4 Tbs. cream cheese   *1 Tbs. flour*
2 Tbs. margarine, melted   *1/4 tsp. cinnamon*

Cut date in half lengthwise, not going through totally so it can be spread open. Add about 1 tsp. of cream cheese and close back to date shape. Put 1 Tbs. margarine in fry pan and heat. Roll dates in remaining margarine then in mixture of brown sugar, flour and cinnamon. Fry quickly on all sides and eat warm.

Cheese Carumba

1 cup grated, crumbled, or diced cheese
4 Tbs. whole wheat flour   *1/4 tsp. cumin*
1/4 - 1/2 tsp. salt   *1 Tbs. cold water*
cayenne or Tabasco to taste

Combine all ingredients. Add more water or more flour if necessary to form a stiff dough. Roll thin and cut into squares. Fry on both sides in an oiled pan. Remove from pan and let sit for a few moments. Shake on more cumin, cayenne or Tabasco as desired.

Popcorn

1 Tbs. oil (margarine will work if you are careful)
1/2 cup popcorn

Heat oil in frying pan with a lid. Add a few kernels of popcorn. When they pop, add popcorn and cover. Place pan over hot coals or stove and shake until popping subsides. Salt popcorn or sprinkle with soy sauce and brewer's yeast. Or add cayenne and cumin to some melted margarine and pour over popcorn.

Roasted nuts and seeds

Heat a fry pan. Add raw nuts or seeds and dry-roast, stirring to prevent burning. Sprinkle with salt or soy sauce.

RECIPE INDEX